Happy Trails

The Story of Two Hikers and Their Path to the New Hampshire Four Thousand Footers and Beyond

Copyright 2011, 2012, 2013 and 2104 by Leonard J. Nyberg, Jr.

All rights reserved. While parts of this book are a compilation of items that are in the public domain, the author's photographs and narrative are all copyrighted; accordingly, no part of those portions of the book may be reproduced, transmitted, transcribed, stored in retrieval systems, or translated into any language by any means whatever without the written permission of the author.

ISBN 9781936711352

Cover Design by Michelle Linell
www.eyedesigngraphics.com

Additional copies of this book may be obtained directly from the author, your local bookstore, on-line or in person from Barnes and Noble or Amazon.com.

Dr. Leonard J. Nyberg, Jr.

125 Savageville Road

Lisbon, NH 03585

Or by email at: nyberg1@roadrunner.com

INDEX

	Page
The Early Years…………………………………………………………..	1
Ham Radio………………………………………………………………..	17
Geology of the White Mountain Batholith……………………………..	24
A New Hiking Companion………………………………………………	26
Failure on Mount Success………………………………………………	33
A Study of Two Peaks in Two Seasons………………………………	45
The 2012 Hiking Season……………………………………………….	49
First Overnight Tent Experience in Forty Years……………………..	80
First Stay in an AMC Hut………………………………………………	96
The Last of the Forty-Eight……………………………………………..	105
AMC Four Thousand Footer Club Award Presentations…………………..	117
BEYOND The White Mountains of NH………………………………..	121
Technical Rock Climbing………………………………………………..	126
Winter Fun…………………………………………………………….......	130
The 2013 Hiking Season……………………………………………….	133
On to Vermont……………………………………………………………	145
On to Maine……………………………………………………………....	165
DONE! (at least for now)...	216

INTRODUCTION

When I first conceived this book my intent was to make it a brief history of my personal hiking experiences; however, although the very first part of this book and one or two other sections focus on my own hiking related activities, it won't take very long for the reader to discover that the story is really about two of us and our wanderings together as a hiking team. In the pursuit of our goal to climb all sixty-seven New England mountain peaks that are in excess of four thousand feet, we have hiked forty-two of them together; and all in two and one-half years. But, I'm getting ahead of myself.

DEDICATION

This book is dedicated to everyone who loves God, the mountains and nature and whose hiking experiences have broadened and enriched their lives; and to my wife Dawn, whose patience and understanding are limitless. A special thanks to Ruth Quilitzch for her time spent correcting all of the grammatical errors that I made in the draft.

"My vicinity affords many good walks, and though I have walked almost every day for so many years, and sometimes for several days together, I have not yet exhausted them. An absolutely new prospect is a great happiness, and I can still get this any afternoon. Two or three hours' walking will carry me to as strange a country as I expect ever to see. A single farm-house which I had not seen before is sometimes as good as the dominions of the king of Dahomey. There is in fact a sort of harmony discoverable between the capabilities of the landscape within a circle of ten miles' radius, or the limits of an afternoon walk, and the three-score years and ten of human life. It will never become quite familiar to you.

So we saunter toward the Holy Land; till one day the sun shall shine more brightly than ever he has done, shall perchance shine into our minds and hearts, and light up our whole lives with a great awakening light, so warm and serene and golden as on a bank-side in Autumn."

Henry David Thoreau – Walking, April 23, 1851

HAPPY TRAILS

"My life has been the poem I would have writ,

But I could not both live and utter it."

Thoreau

Dad Fishing in Wood River

My mom and dad graduated from high school together in 1932, after which time my dad worked several jobs in sales and my mom entered nursing school. My father was a natural salesman; he had the gift of gab and a personality that would have allowed him to enter a room full of total strangers and in an hour or so be friends with all of them.

Although he was successful in sales, I think that he would have preferred to be in the outdoors. Several of his letters to my mother were written on stationery from the State Commissioners of Inland Fisheries. Because of his love of fishing, I really think that he really would have liked being a game warden. During their courtship dad spent considerable time at Bungalow Village, on the west shore of Newfound Lake, in Bristol, New Hampshire. Mom continued her nursing career; here she is on the left on the roof of the hospital with one of her classmates. As "probationers," they could only wear black stockings.

On July 6, 1934 while at Bungalow Village, he wrote a letter to my mother: *"....the one and only thing that I miss here honey and that is you honest. Gee if you were here it would positively be 100% and better....I would certainly rather spend my honeymoon up here than anything else...."*

The two were married in 1935 and did, in fact, spend their honeymoon at Bungalow Village. I was born the following year. In the early years we did a lot of camping and, at a very early age, I can remember camping at the Dolly Copp campground, on Route 16 just north of Pinkham Notch. My dad pitched a tent and he and my mom slept there; I spent many nights in the back of our "beach-wagon," aka "woody."

Over the next few years we spent much, if not all of our summer vacation at Bungalow Village on Newfound Lake in Bristol, NH. I discovered a trail in back of our cabin and followed it up to the top of a hill that I named "Mt. Cello," an elevation of about 950 feet, from which there was a fine view of the lake. I frequently hiked to the "summit" and once in a while coaxed my mom, dad and sister to join me. The hike was pretty easy, as the elevation above the lake level was about three hundred and sixty feet. I hiked that trail almost every day and sometimes several times a day. At left are dad, mom and my sister on Mt. Cello.

Nearby Mt. Cardigan (3,121') presented one of my first mountaineering experiences and since my first ascent I have hiked this peak many times and on many, if not all of its trails, including the Manning Trail, the Holt Trail, the Mowglis Trail, and, more recently, the West Ridge Trail.

My father - and even my grandparents enjoyed hiking. My father's younger brother Elmer was an avid hiker and hiked most, if not all of the Long Trail in Vermont as well as many peaks in the White Mountains of New Hampshire. In the photograph at right my dad, grandmother and grandfather are standing in front of the summit house on Mt. Monadnock (3,165'), in Ringe, New Hampshire, c.1930.

These adventures sparked my interest in hiking at a very early age, however; it was not until high school that it became a little more serious. I also believe that my father's love for the outdoors was greatly influential in my life and my love for outdoors and the mountains.

My earliest hiking companion was Ray Barrie who lived on my street about three houses away. We hiked together for a couple of years and he was so flexible that I could call him on a Friday at about three o'clock and ask: "..hey Ray, want to go hiking this weekend?" Response: "Sure." Reply: "OK, I'll pick you up in ten minutes…" "OK."

Here is a photograph of Ray and me along with Skipper, my next-door neighbor. Ray is on the far left with the sun glasses and Skipper is in the middle wearing my cowboy hat; I'm wearing the same shirt that I was wearing in the photo taken at the summit of Mt. Katahdin. The photo was taken around 1953 or 1954 and the place was my parents' living room in Rumford, RI.

It was interesting that Ray seemed to have taken his flexible attitude from his parents who were also good friends with my parents. We lived in the town of Rumford, RI (now part of East Providence) and frequently, on a warm summer evening, my parents would crave some ice cream – their favorite spot was Bliss Brothers Dairy in nearby Attleboro, MA, about twenty minutes away. My dad would call Ray's dad and ask if they would like to take a ride up to Bliss Brothers for ice cream – the answer was invariably YES. "OK, we'll pick you up in ten minutes…"

Ray and I started our hiking adventures on Mt. Chocorua (3,475'), where we camped near the foot of the Piper Trail. We had very little camping equipment of our own and used the tent that my folks had used for years along with their Coleman gas stove and lantern, equipment that we would continue to use for some time to come.

This is a photo of our campsite at the base of the trail; the old tent can be seen in the rear center and the Coleman gas stove at lower right. It looks like I must of had cooking detail that day.

Here I am on the summit – back then I always wore the cowboy hat when I hiked. Now I almost always wear my Boeing 727 cap.

Mt. Chocorua – Me   **Mt. Chocorua - Ray**

Our first five thousand foot peak was Mt. Katahdin (5,267') which we approached from the Katahdin Creek Campground. There were four of us in our party; I don't remember the other two, but we had a great time. Our tent, of course, was the old canvas tent of my parents and we slept one on each side. During the first night, we were rudely awakened by a curious deer that actually attempted to enter the tent and in doing so stepped on the occupant next to the door on the front side. I grabbed my camera and tried to take a photo but it was too dark; the next day, however, we were graced by the presence of the buck who had attempted a late night break-in.

Happily, the buck exhibited no fear and we hand fed it candy bars and bread – in return he allowed us to rub his antlers which, at that time, were in "velvet." The following morning we headed up the trail to the summit – what a view! The photo at right is of the happy campers, a little out of focus, at the summit cairn. That's me on the left with the cowboy hat and Ray in the middle with his signature straw hat.

Logging operations were in full swing at the time of our hike and the logs were jammed up at Ripogenus Dam as loggers directed the logs down the chute at the left side of the dam. As the logs shot down the chute it sounded like rolls of thunder. The river below the dam where the logs are being sent, is the West Branch of the Penobscot River, one of my dad's favorite salmon fishing spots in Maine. Several years ago I hired a guide and fished the river at a spot known as the "Big Eddy."

As I mentioned, our family spent almost all of our vacations at Bungalow Village until we found rental cottages on the east shore of the lake; we moved to that location until 1953 when, while boating on the lake, we spotted a for sale sign on a vacant lot on Whittemore Point. After some negotiation my dad made the purchase and we spent the remainder of the summer clearing the lot by hand. The following year we built a two bedroom cottage, continued to clear, constructed a driveway, built a dock and boat ramp and settled in for the season. For the next several years we hauled gravel, pounded nails and moved rocks from the water so we could have a small beach area.

The cottage was located about an hour from good hiking spots in Franconia Notch and along the Kangamagus Highway, then just an unimproved gravel road. We used the cottage as a "jumping off" spot for many years of hiking adventures.

During the summer of 1954, my friend Ray and I were councilors at a YMCA day camp in nearby Massachusetts where we met Fred Maker, the father of one of the campers. Fred was a member of the Appalachian Mountain Club (AMC) trail crew in Whitefield, NH, and heard of our interest in hiking. He spent quite a lot of time with us telling tales of hikes that he had been on and explaining some of the details regarding possible hikes for us.

We asked for a plan for a hike to the Presidential Range and he was kind enough to not only write out details for us, but gave us a copy of the 1934 AMC White Mountain Guide.

I still have the guide AND his notes:

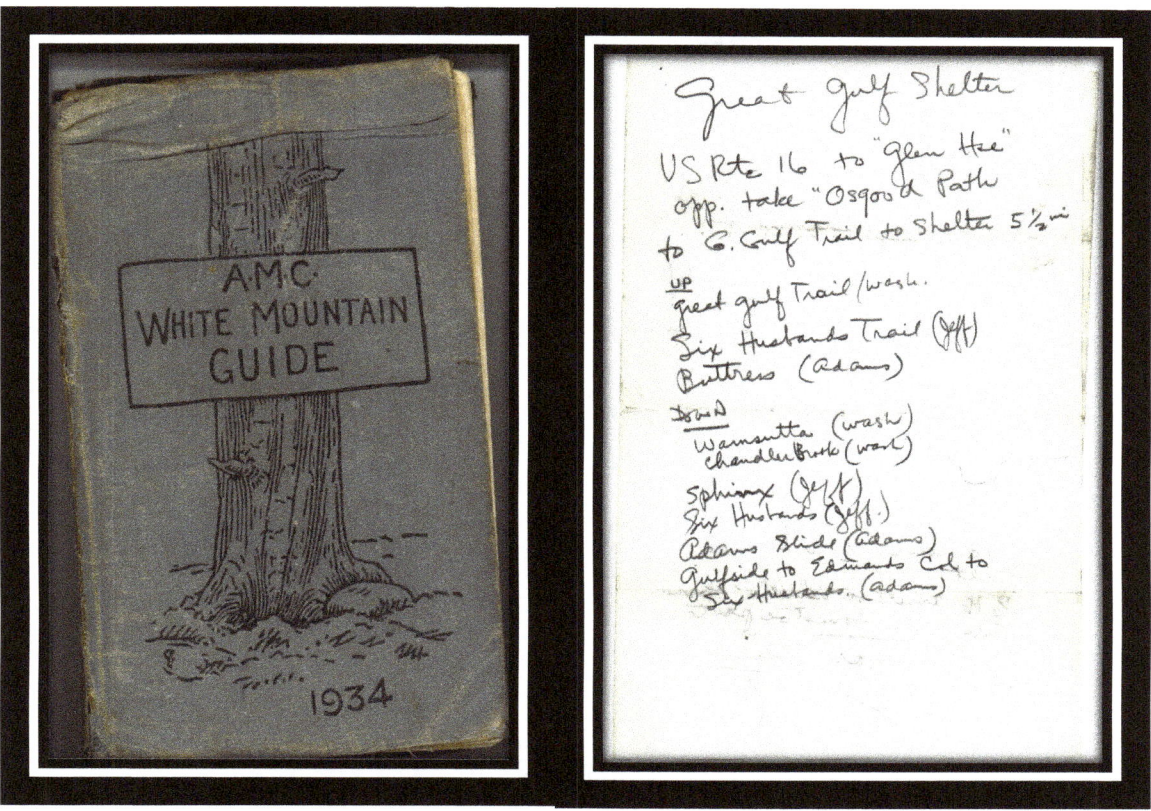
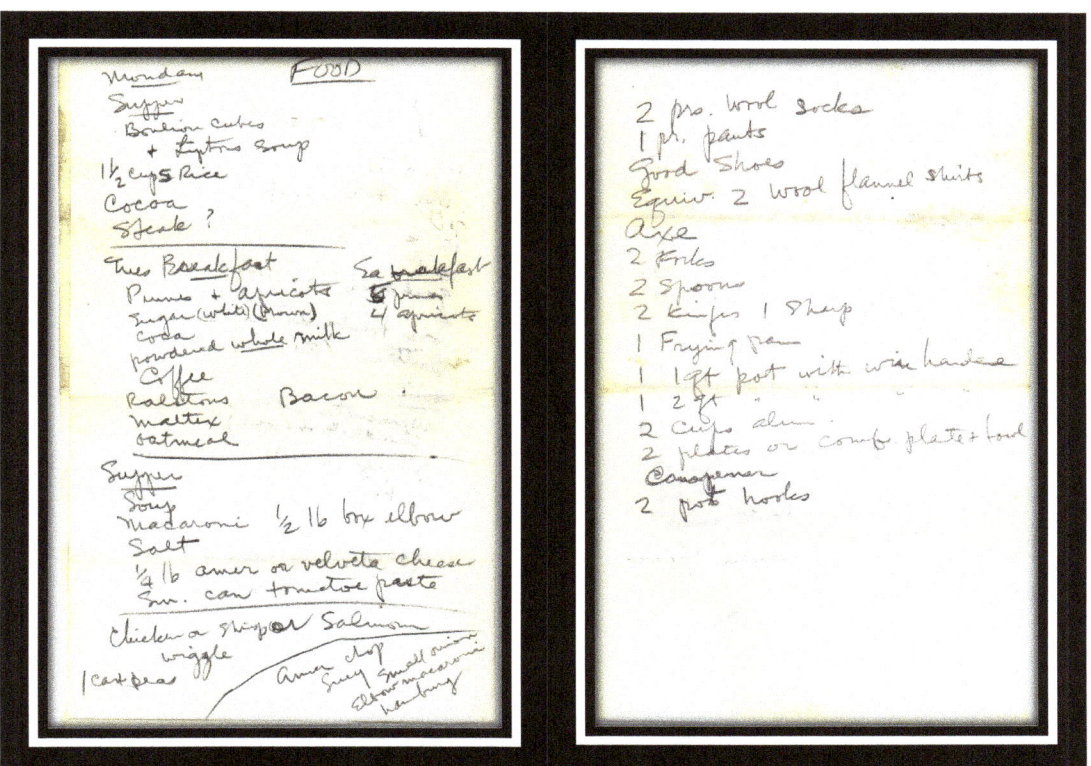

The end of this hike found us on the slope of Mt. Washington (6,288'), and Ray and I descended via the Great Gulf Trail and decided to overnight at Spaulding Lake (4,250'), at the foot of the headwall. There was a kind of a "cave" there and we spread out our sleeping bags, prepared dinner and got ourselves ready for the night. At about midnight we heard claps of thunder and saw flashes of lightning and it wasn't long before we discovered that our "cave" leaked. So, we packed up our stuff and put on bathing suits for the trek down to the Great Gulf Shelter (3,250'). The trip was about 1.3 miles and the only light that we had was from very frequent lightning flashes. When we arrived at the shelter we were completely soaked and there was no dry wood – we lit candles and cooked some packaged soup over the candles.

The Great Gulf Shelter was located southwest of the junction of the Great Gulf and Wamsutta Trails. It was an open log shelter and could accommodate up to twenty-two persons. A rather large stone fireplace was located directly in front and although hikers could find a few cooking utensils from time to time, there were no amenities. We took advantage of this shelter for many more excursions up Mt. Washington and other peaks in the Presidential Range.

Although I moved out of the area, I never lost touch with Ray. As a matter of fact, currently we communicate frequently via the Internet and although it has been over twelve years since we have seen each other in person we have a friendship that transcends distance;. our families had that same friendship. Ray's mom passed away on August 14, 2000 and I was asked to play the organ at the Service of Thanksgiving to God for the Life of Ethel E. Barrie held at Newman Congregational Church in Rumford, RI. This was the same church that my mom and dad attended; my dad was a deacon there – I also played memorial services there for both my mom and dad.

After the services for Ray's mom, I received the following note from Ray and Carolyn:

Years and miles can't change the loyalty of true friendship. That's what it seems to be with the Nyberg's and the Barrie's'

How can we thank you for the gift of your talent and your donation to mom's Memorial? No words can express it. Just thanks!!

Ray and Carolyn

In 1962 I got married and my wife became my camping and hiking companion; as a matter of fact we spent our honeymoon at our cottage on the lake. During the following years, we hiked many of the New Hampshire Four Thousand Footers, and spent many nights in the open log style shelters that were scattered throughout the White Mountains. The Wilderness Trail was one of our favorites and we frequently camped at the shelters located at the site of former camps used by loggers. The Franconia Brook Shelter along the Franconia Brook was a frequent campsite that we used, but our favorite was the shelter located at what is now the 13 Falls campsite (photo below left). We were joined by our German Shepherd dog Snus, who was a hiking companion for many years.

One of our first hiking adventures took us to Mt. Washington via the Tuckerman Ravine Trail and an overnight at the Hermit Lake shelter. The shelter, which I believe no longer exists, was built in 1953 and accommodated about sixty people – it was built in the shape of a wide-angled "U." The photo below right is of Tuckerman's Ravine from Hermit Lake.

Late in the afternoon I built a pretty good fire so we could make some dinner, after which I noted that the three young ladies next to us were making futile attempts to build one of their own. I suggested that since we had finished dinner they were invited to use our fire for their dinner, they readily agreed. Later, when their male hiking companions returned for dinner the men were so impressed with the fire they commented on it. The ladies, of course, told them that they hadn't built the fire but it was mine and they were just using it. The men were quite thankful and invited me to join them in a cold beer and handed me a 16 oz. can of Budweiser.

Meanwhile, one of the other campers saw the beer and inquired as to how much money it would take to purchase one – the answer was that none was for sale. The offer increased dramatically but the answer remained the same. So, the camper headed down the trail to the parking area in search of a store where he could purchase his own; sadly when he got down to the parking area he discovered that he had left his car keys back at the shelter so, he hiked back to the shelter and retrieved his car keys. He then hiked back to the parking area, drove to Gorham, purchased his beer, returned to Pinkham Notch, parked and hiked back to the shelter, arriving well after dark. I thought later that if I had known that the beer was that important to him, I would gladly have given him mine.

Almost There! **Finally Made It!**

The photos above were all taken in September, 1962 while we were on the hike described earlier. This was the first significant hike that my new bride accompanied me on and she was somewhat perturbed when we finally arrived at the summit and she spotted a woman who was wearing high heeled shoes – evidently just up on the Cog Railroad.

During the next couple of years we camped all around New England as well as Virginia, North and South Carolina, Tennessee and Georgia.

During the summer of 1963 we were camped along the Blue Ridge Parkway and were befriended by a National Park Ranger named Zeke who took us on numerous hikes in the area. One day he told us that he had to check on the former camp of President Hoover, a place called Rapidan Camp, and asked if we would like to go – at that time the camp was off limits to visitors. Of course we agreed and Zeke drove us in his Jeep and through a gated area to the camp. President Hoover was an avid fly fisherman and the brooks that ran through the camp were stocked with trout by the Department of the Interior.

Zeke, shown at right, parked the Jeep and we hiked into the camp area. According to him, the president's criteria was distance from Washington, privacy, at least two trout streams and being at an altitude above the mosquito line. Well, the camp was private with two trout streams; however, I can't vouch for it being above the mosquito line. We looked at the president's cabin, and the cabins for the visiting dignitaries. It was said that most of the fishing was done outside the camp grounds as the fish within the grounds were fed to such an extent that they were close to being tame. Sadly, the photographs that I took of the buildings are so dark that they are virtually impossible to make out.

In the fall of 1965 we resumed our hiking in New Hampshire and the next adventure was Mt. Lafayette (5,260'), the Franconia Ridge Trail and Cannon Mountain. We camped at the Lafayette Campground and headed up the Old Bridle Path to the summit. From the summit we headed south on the Franconia Ridge Trail, crossing Mt. Lincoln (5,108"), Little Haystack Mtn. (4,513'), Mt. Liberty (4,459') and Mt. Flume (4,328'). We descended via the Flume Slide Trail and hiked the highway back to the campground.

At left: My rather crude hiking notes describing the overall plan which took us to Mt. Lafayette and the Franconia Ridge Trail to Mt. Flume, then to Lonesome Lake and Cannon Mountain via Lonesome Lake and Kinsman Ridge Trails, returning via the Hi-Cannon Trail.

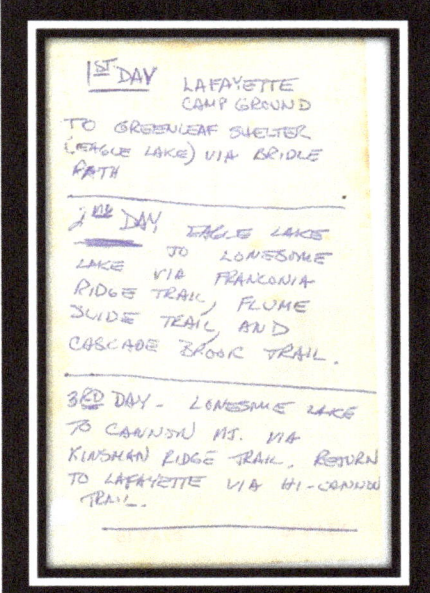

At the summit of Mt. Lafayette

The Franconia Ridge Trail

Later we hiked Mt. Lafayette again; this time we took the Falling Waters Trail and camped at Eagle Lake (at right), a small pond not too far from the AMC Greenleaf Hut. Since on that trip we only planned to be camped for one night, we took wine, steak, potatoes and a little charcoal – a bit extravagant I admit, but it was a very enjoyable evening none-the-less.

Our next hike took us to the west side of Franconia Notch and hiked the Lonesome Lake Trail again to the Kinsman Ridge Trail and headed south over the Cannon Balls and overnighted at the Kinsman Pond Shelter – we stayed at this shelter several times during the next year or so. One night a young man on one of his first hikes, was cooking dinner over a portable stove and while in the process of cooking he accidentally kicked the stove over and his dinner was gone! Fortunately, we had enough food and were more than happy to give him some of ours. The following day we scaled both North (4,293') and South (4,358') Kinsman Mountains and returned to the Lafayette Campground via the Fishin Jimmy Trail.

During the fall of 1963 it was announced that I had been appointed organist and choirmaster of the Mathewson Street Methodist Church in Providence, RI. The church had a volunteer choir but it was supported by a paid quartet - the alto was Florence Caldwell. Florence had two teenage boys and when they discovered that I liked to hike they asked if I would plan a trip for them.

Since I was pretty familiar with the routes, I suggested that we attack the Presidential Range and establish a base camp at the Great Gulf Shelter; accordingly, I drafted a somewhat energetic plan that included Mts. Madison, Adams, Jefferson, Clay and Washington.

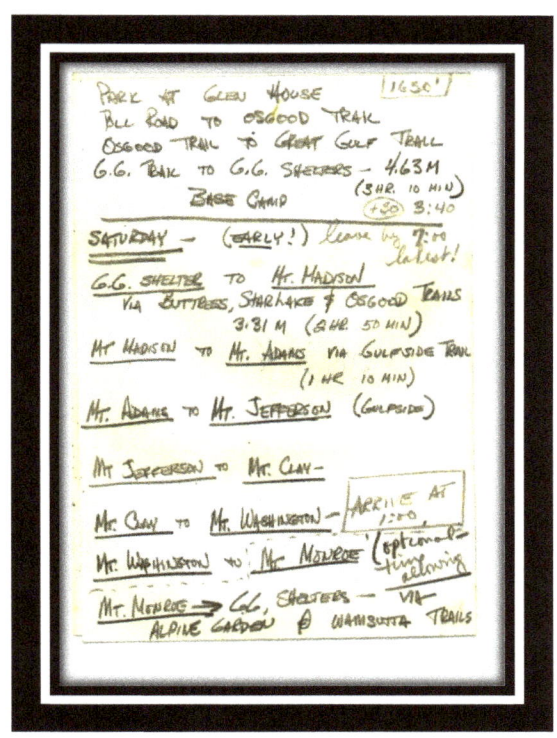

The boys were excited and on July 29, 1965, Florence's husband Al wrote the letter shown at left:

Intestinal fortitude we will develop as we need it. Spirit of adventure we have. Will meet you at Newfound Lake on Friday August 6th at 10 AM. Send card to designate exact place.

We met as agreed and started our adventure. Sadly, after reaching the tree-line, Florence found that she had a fear of heights and went back to the Great Gulf shelter for the remainder of the weekend. Other than that, it was an enjoyable hike.

Another adventure found us on the south side of the Kancamagus Highway and an attempt at Mt. Osceola. We stayed overnight at the Greeley Pond Shelter. The next morning we headed up the East Peak (4,156') and, after reaching the summit, decided to save the main summit for another day. The photo at right was taken from the East Peak – Mt. Osceola summit had a fire tower on the summit at that time.

We then decided to head to Crawford Notch and mapped a trip over the Ethan Pond Trail into Zealand Notch and on to Zeacliff. We left our car at the Zealand Trailhead and my parents drove us over to Crawford's where we struck out for Ethan Pond – we planned to stay overnight at the Shelter there. Unfortunately, when we arrived we found that a troop of Boy Scouts had taken over the shelter and we had to fend for ourselves.

Scrap wood, an axe and small pack saw allowed me to construct a small lean-to where we could spend the night. I was pretty proud of the results and the best part was that I didn't have to cut down one tree. After I built the frame, I made a roof with our waterproof ponchos.

This experience prompted me to purchase a tent and carry it on future hikes just in case shelters that we planned on were occupied. The photograph at left is of the tent pitched at Sawyer Pond during our hike to Mt. Carrigan.

The tent was lightweight and easy to set up but it didn't have a rain fly so, in late fall or when it rained, the tent had a tendency to "sweat." But, it served us well and fit two people and a German Shepherd dog snugly, but comfortably. We used this tent for many years and in three out of four seasons.

In 1969 I was a captain for a regional airline and transferred to Burlington, Vermont; accordingly, we purchased a home in the small town of Worcester (population 505) and I commuted from there to the Burlington Airport. Although we did continue to hike in New Hampshire to some extent, I joined the Green Mountain Club and did a lot of hiking in Vermont.

Since one of our stops was Montpelier, I became friendly with a member of the FAA team who worked at the Montpelier Flight Service Station; his name was Ron Parker and he had the same love for hiking that I did, particularly during the winter. I volunteered to "adopt" the Montclair Glen Lodge in Wind Gap on Camel's Hump and, during the months when there was no snow, I trekked up once a week to check on the shelter and pack out any trash that had accumulated there. During the winter months I hiked up on  snowshoes once every couple of weeks. That's me above with my German Shepherd "Snus."

Page 15

Ron lived in nearby Middlesex and the Worcester Mountain Range was directly north of my home and east of Ron's. Had the range not been there, I would have looked directly at Mt. Mansfield in Stowe. Although the range was not a particularly significant one, we frequently hiked it, especially during the winter months. We established no trails but set up compass coordinates to locate water and potential campsites.

In the photograph above (c. 1969), Ron is shown with my three Shepherds - Snus and Bambi are with Ron, Major is at lower left – the photograph was taken on the slopes of Mt. Worcester (3,274'). The dogs loved to hike and would break the trail for hours; however, on our way back I frequently felt them on the tail of my snowshoes. Snus was a ninety pound female; Major weighed over one hundred pounds and Bambi was their offspring.

Our hiking activities came to a halt around 1968 when my wife and I separated and then divorced. The following year my dad died and, in 1970, I moved back to Rhode Island to care for my mother. In 1996 I re-married and subsequently moved to New Hampshire where we established a municipal consulting firm. Although we were living in the White Mountains, our business didn't allow much, if any, time for hiking.

In addition to my interest in hiking, I am an avid amateur radio operator. I first got involved in 1949 and although there have been a few intervals over the years when I have not been on the air, I am currently very active.

Sometime around 2006, I met a fellow ham radio operator who had carried portable ham radio equipment to the nearby summits to communicate with fellow hams around the country. Our first hike was to the summit of Mt. Moosilauke (4,802') where we set-up and communicated with about a dozen or more fellow hams in New York, New Jersey, Massachusetts, Connecticut, Vermont and Canada. We did the same with other local peaks, Blueberry Mountain being one of our favorites.

This is a photograph of me at the summit of Mt. Moosilauke during one of our ham radio excursions. On this trip, during the month of October, we used the summit sign as a support for the beam antenna that we used to communicate on 2 meter single-sideband. Later, I purchased a truly lightweight multi-band transceiver which gave me the ability to transmit on both the High Frequency and Very High Frequency bands.

I currently operate under the call sign W1LJN and, although still very active in ham radio, no longer hike with radio equipment.

About one-third of the way up the Benton Trail there is a wonderful spot to stop, take a rest and enjoy the beautiful views to the north and east. I always stop at this place, both on ascent and descent.

In this photograph the moon is showing itself just above the ridge directly east of my resting place. It was during the month of October and the day was cold and windy. I stayed too long at the summit and at the rest spot and noted that the sun was beginning to set in the west.

I strapped on my pack and, as I stepped onto the trail, it appeared that a tree was on fire; however, it was the blazing sunset reflecting in the break of a pine tree.

I continued on the trail and hiked the last mile or so in the dark.

With flashlights the portion of the hike after sunset really *w*asn't much of a problem, but the crossing of Tunnel Brook in the dark was a challenge.

All's well that ends well – the crossing was uneventful and the day was more than enjoyable.

Another favorite hike is Blueberry Mountain (2,662') in Benton, NH. The trail that I use most is the Blueberry Mountain Trail from the Long Pond Road. Another access is from Lime Kiln Road on the west side of the mountain; I have only hiked this part of the trail once.

This is a relatively easy hike and the distance from the Long Pond Road to the summit is 1.7 miles; from the other direction the distance is just over a mile longer. The views from the summit are pleasant and there is considerable ledge on upper parts of the mountain. Just below the summit on the northwest ledges you can pick out mountains in Vermont.

We have set up radio equipment and antennae in several areas of the upper ledges and, although we frequently used a beam antenna, more recently we have suspended wire antennae from tree branches. We have talked to friends as far south as New Jersey and Pennsylvania, and as far west as Michigan.

In the photograph at right I'm pictured with one of our VHF radio set-ups on the summit of Blueberry Mountain (2,662'). This remains one of my favorite hikes and, although I have not hiked there during the winter months, I love to visit during the other three seasons. My favorite spot is about two hundred feet below the summit – the view of Mt. Moosilauke from there is gorgeous.

In this photograph I am operating on 40 meter AM. You can see the wire antenna above me and the feed line coming down behind me. The hand-held transceiver dimensions are 5.31" x 1.5" x 6.5" and the weight including the battery and the microphone, is 2.58 lbs. as opposed to the 18 lb. weight of the battery, radio and microphone previously carried. A portion of the Mt. Moosilauke ridgeline can be seen behind me.

This photo is my very favorite view; it was taken from a ledge about two hundred feet below the summit of Blueberry Mountain, looking northeasterly at Mt. Moosilauke. It is interesting to note that from this location South Peak (4,523'), on the right, appears higher than the North Peak (4,802') – I refer to this as somewhat of an "optical delusion."

This is an example of the majesty of God's creation and I never cease to stop and enjoy it and be thankful.

"I wander with the pollen of dawn upon my trail. Beauty surrounding me, with it I wander.

Beauty behind me, with it I wander."   The mountain chants of the Navaho

In the photo below, I'm enjoying this view from my favorite resting spot – sometimes I even doze off for a little while, it's a very tranquil place and a great source of mental comfort and relaxation.

Early last summer I convinced my wife Dawn to join me for a hike up Blueberry Mountain. I wanted her to get some idea of why I enjoyed hiking this mountain as much as I do.

Thankfully, the wildflower season was in full bloom and she got a chance to see so many variations and in so many numbers. We were both particularly impressed with the number of Pink Lady's Slippers (*cypripedium acaule*), we stopped counting at more than three hundred – I had never in my life seen so many. In the photograph above there are more than twenty-five.

The other wildflower that we saw in abundance was the Pink Azalea (*Rhododendron nudiflorum*). This is a beautiful flower that ranges from New England south to South Carolina. The Latin name *nudiflorum*, means "naked-flowered" and is named as such because the flowers often appear before the leaves have matured.

My hiking friend and I hiked frequently and, although we didn't do much in the four thousand foot category, we did do a lot of bushwhacking and had a lot of fun doing so. There came a time during the 2011 season that we had a falling out and no longer able to hike together; however, that did not stop me from hiking and I renewed my quest to conquer the New Hampshire Four Thousand Footers. Since I didn't have a hiking companion and my wife doesn't enjoy hiking, I was forced to hike solo.

My first solo hike was Mt. Garfield (4,500'). Then North Twin (4,761') and South Twin (4,902') followed. On the Garfield hike I found myself on the Gale River Trail instead of the Garfield Trail – this added a couple of extra miles and a few more hours to the day but it was well worth the extra effort.

At left is a photograph of the AMC Galehead Hut with South Twin Mountain in upper left. The day was ideal for hiking and, although it was a long one, I did meet a fellow hiker on the way back down the Garfield Trail and he was kind enough to give me a ride back to my car when we got back to the end of the trail.

From the summit of Mt. Garfield there are magnificent views of the Pemigewasset Wilderness to the south and Mt. Lafayette and the Franconia Ridge Trail to the west.

Owl's Head Mountain – looking south **Mt. Lincoln and the Franconia Ridge- looking southwest**

North and South Twin Mountains were next on my list and it was another gorgeous day for hiking. When I solo hike I carry a cell phone so I can keep my wife informed as to where I am and confirm that I am alive and well.

From a ledgey lookout just east of the north peak, the views toward Mt. Washington are outstanding.

This is a photograph looking east from the lookout. Mt. Hale can be seen in the foreground and Mt. Washington in the distance.

From the same ledge there is a great view of South Twin and the portion the ridge that the trail follows from North Twin.

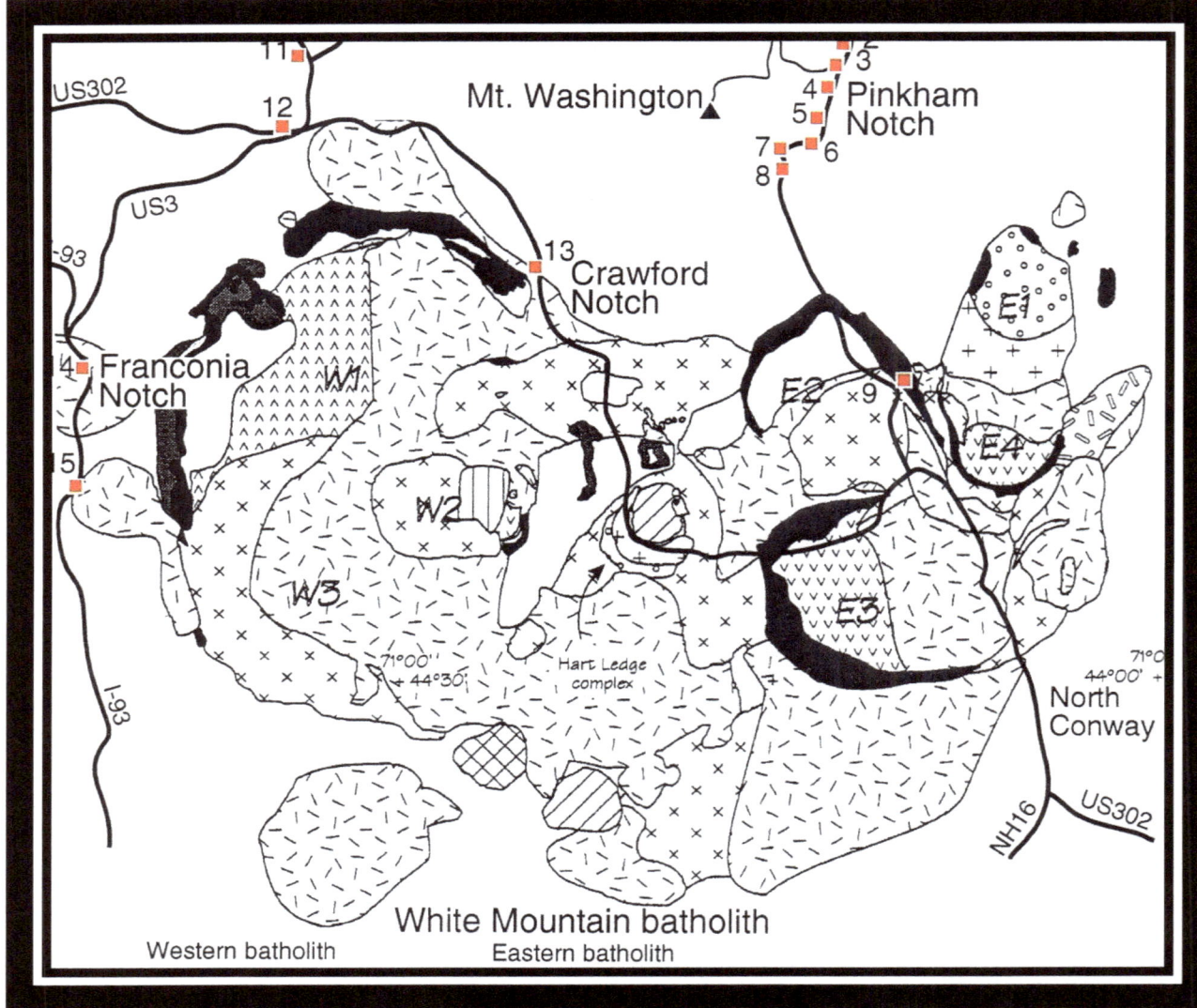

The Geology of the White Mountain batholith (after Creasy, 1974; Osberg et al,. 1978)

As I hiked along the Garfield Ridge Trail I didn't realize that I was walking along the ridge of what was once a volcano. The black arc at the upper left of this diagram extends from Mt. Willey in Crawford's to the Franconia Ridge in Franconia Notch. The center of the arc is the caldera, or what is defined as a large, basin-like depression resulting from the explosion or collapse of the center of a volcano. This area is essentially the Pemigewasset Wilderness.

The black arc is depicted as Porphyritic quartz syenite and, according to the USGS, dates back to the Jurassic period – 208-144 million years ago. It's amazing what one can learn by hiking the White Mountains of New Hampshire.

Another View of the White Mountain Batholith

From *The Geology of New Hampshire* by Marland P. Billings

The center of the complex is midway between Mts. Carrigan and Bond

In this photograph I'm at the summit of South Twin Mountain. While on the summit I met a Canadian couple who asked if I would take a photograph of them, in return they took several of me.

I next attacked Mt. Hale (4,054') and hiked the Hale Brook Trail up and the Lend-a-Hand and Zealand Trails back to the car; the round trip is about twelve miles. I thought that the Lend-a-Hand Trail was aptly named and was rather pleased with myself for not choosing this trail for the ascent. I later did a little research and discovered that the mountain was named for Edward Everett Hale, an American author, historian and Unitarian clergyman. His motto, *"Look up and not down, look forward and not back, look out*

and not in, and lend a hand", was the basis for the formation of the Lend a Hand clubs and for the naming of the Lend-a-Hand Trail.

In late July, 2011, I solo hiked Mt. Tom (4,051'). My plan was to solo Mts. Tom, Field, Willey and Avalon. While at the summit I met a young man from Massachusetts who was kind enough to take a photo of me at the summit. The conversation got to what plans I had for the day. I told him that I planned to hike four peaks that day.

His reply was that he was only planning to hike three and not go as far as Mt. Willey. Somehow the conversation got to age and when I told him that I was seventy-five, he exclaimed that if I could do all four at my age, then he (age 49) could do all four as well – "….can I join you?" he asked. I told him that I would welcome the company, so we hiked together for the rest of the day. When we arrived at the summit of Mt. Willey (4,285'), we caught up with two couples who we had passed several times on the trail – they were feeding the "Grey-Jays" that frequented the area and were always on the prowl for a handout. My newly found friend Rick decided to give it a try, and our summit friends provided him with some food to feed our feathered friends.

For some reason, probably because it was such a surprise for them to see a 75 year old senior citizen hiking the four thousand foot New Hampshire peaks, the ladies in the party wanted to have their photograph taken with me at the summit, and, of course, I obliged.

Later, when my mother-in-law saw the photograph, her question was: "…how much did you have to pay those women to have your picture taken with them?" Obviously it was my charming personality that prompted the request.

Rick and I backtracked to Mt. Field (4,340') and then headed down the Avalon Link to the short side spur that led us to the summit of Mt. Avalon (3,432').

Here's Rick taking a well-deserved break at Avalon's summit. From here we had a great view of the AMC Center and the RR station where we had parked our vehicles.

Here I am at the summit.

After a brief stay at the summit we continued on to the parking area at Crawford Notch. Rick indicated that he would like to hike with me again and we exchanged phone numbers and email addresses and agreed to meet again. We hiked the remainder of the season together, and completed fourteen peaks before ending the season in December after our hike up Mt. North Tripyramid (4,180').

I was indeed very fortunate to have met Rick; he is a great hiking companion and keeps a good watch over his much older hiking buddy. A good example was during one of our hikes to Middle Tripyramid (4,140') and in spite of an early morning start to our hike, the Sabbaday Brook was quite high because of recent rains; accordingly, we had to bushwhack much of the way up because some of the brook crossings were impossible to negotiate. When we arrived at the last crossing we were on the east side of the brook and it was necessary to cross here to continue up the trail to the summit. We split up and, after inspecting the shore both north and south of our position, failed to find a satisfactory place to cross without getting the "old man" wet. Well, Rick found a solution:

I had hiked East Osceola (4,156') back in 1965 but never made it to the summit of Osceola. So Rick and I met on the "Kanc" early on the 3rd of August, left my car at the Greely Pond Trailhead and then drove to Waterville Valley and left his truck at the parking area in Thornton Gap off the Tripoli Road. We ascended the Mt. Osceola Trail and when we reached the summit (4,340') it was quite cloudy and there wasn't much of a view; however, it wasn't too long before the clouds dissipated and we began to get some of the views. The photo above shows the East Peak with the clouds just starting to break.

Back in 1965 when I had hiked the East Peak there was a fire tower on the summit of Osceola; all that remains now are the concrete blocks that formed part of the foundation of the tower.

Rick Avoiding the "Chimney"   **Me at the Summit of East Osceola**

On August 12th Rick and I met at the parking area at the "hairpin curve" on the Kancamagus Highway in preparation for our hike to North Hancock (4,420') and South Hancock (4,319'). We started early and headed north on the Hancock Notch Trail. At 1.8 miles we switched to the Cedar Brook Trail and 0.7 miles later the Hancock Loop Trail. The first part of the trail was relatively level and followed the North Fork of the Hancock Brook. Soon the trail steepened a bit and, shortly after, we descended and crossed a dry brook bed before ascending rather steeply. We paralleled the Arrow Slide, a rock slide below the ridge joining the two peaks.

We soon reached the wooded summit of North Hancock, posed for photographs for a moment and then turned north toward the outlook which affords great views to the south to the Sandwich Range and Mt. Osceola.

We then turned south and followed the Ridge Link Trail to the south peak which, like its twin, is wooded with no view.

However, there is a short side path that leads to an outlook that affords views of the Sawyer River Valley.

In the photos above, Rick and I are holding a piece of birchbark where someone had written "I love it here!" on the backside.

On August 18th I fulfilled a long-time goal and, along with Hank Peterson, ascended Mt. Success (3,565') in Berlin, NH. The purpose for the hike was to locate the site of the 1954 crash of a Northeast Airlines Douglas DC-3. The fact that I am a DC-3 captain intensified the hike for me.

We drove to the Success Trail trailhead and proceeded along the trail with a stop at a short loop trail that led to a spectacular ledge that provided excellent views of the Presidential Range and the summit of Mt. Success.

At 2.4 miles the trail meets the Mahoosuc Trail; the summit was reached in 0.6 miles via this trail. From the summit the trail continues in a generally southwesterly direction and crosses, via a wooden walkway, a bog area loaded with wild cranberries, As the trail begins to descend, bushwhacking becomes necessary and after a while we came across a boundary trail which eventually led to the crash site.

Northeast Airlines Flight 792 departed Boston for Berlin, NH with intermediate stops at Concord and Laconia. The plane crashed during a snowstorm and was located on Mt. Success, about 100 feet below the summit elevation, a couple of days later. The pilot was severely injured and the co-pilot and observer were killed; the stewardess and passengers survived.

Here is Hank "signing-in" for his fourteenth visit to the site. It was my first visit and as a certified DC-3 Captain I was able to identify many items. It is amazing how much of the aircraft remains after being exposed to the elements for over fifty-five years.

After the crash a salvage path was constructed. That path was used by hikers for many years after and AMC Guidebooks in the 1960's describe the route – that route now is overgrown, making finding the site a bit of a challenge.

Here is a rather inglorious photograph of me inspecting the lavatory section of the plane.

We spent a couple of hours at the site before heading back to the summit, trail and our vehicle.

Wild Cranberries

Wild Blueberries

Here's Hank negotiating one of the more challenging parts of the trail.

Here's one last view from the summit before heading home.

On October 10th I packed up and headed to Jefferson for a solo hike up Mt. Waumbek (4,006'). The day was pleasant and the trail, although moderate right from the beginning, was pleasant.

Along the path were two interesting structures that formerly provided water to the Waumbek Hotel that once existed near the trailhead. The first structure was a stone reservoir and the second a stone spring that provided the water. Remnants of the iron piping that conveyed the water could be seen along the trail.

In order to reach the summit of Mt. Waumbek, it was necessary to scale the peak of Mt. Starr King (3,907') first. The mountain is named after Thomas Starr King, the author of **"The White Hills; Their Legends, Landscape and Poetry."**

The summit is wooded and there are no views; within about twenty meters is a clearing where an old cabin once stood – all that remains is the fireplace.

The building was once a private shelter and was destroyed sometime between 1960 and 1966.

From this clearing the trail re-enters the woods and, following the ridge that joins the two peaks, eventually reaches the summit of Mt. Waumbek at the junction of the Starr King Trail and the Kilkenny Ridge Trail.

As with Mt. Starr King, the summit of Mt. Waumbek is treed and viewless; however, there is a viewpoint about thirty meters from the summit that affords views of the Presidentials to the southeast.

The viewpoint below the summit consists of a small clearing with somewhat limited views; it is a pleasant spot to have lunch and relax before the return hike.

Me at the Trail Sign at the Summit   **Mts. Starr King and Waumbek from Route 2**

Back in July, I solo hiked Mt. Hale (4,054'), but Rick had not done it, so I agreed to hike it again with him on October 31st. We met at the Hale Brook Trail trailhead early in the morning and headed up the trail. Our plan was to hike the Hale Brook Trail to the summit and then descend the Lend-a-Hand Trail to the Zealand Hut and return via the Zealand Trail.

The lower part of the trail was dry but at about the three thousand foot level we ran into snow and ice.

For the most part the snow was less than six inches deep (left); however, there were spots where the trail looked like a frozen brook (below). In spite of that during the entire ascent we were still able to proceed without the need of crampons or MICROspikes.

Rick arrived at the summit about fifteen minutes before me and, when I arrived, he was shirtless and talking to someone on his cellphone.

Well, at the summit I elected to keep my shirt on and Rick decided to get dressed for the occasion. There had been a fire tower on the summit at one time but all that was left were the steps and evidence of the foundation. Over the years the trees had grown to a point that there was no view; evidently some enterprising hikers had built a pile of stones to get a view; sadly, even from the top of the pile, the view no longer exists.

We descended to the AMC Zealand Hut via the Lend-a-Hand Trail. Here is Rick resting on the front porch, enjoying some hot chocolate that he had in his pack.

Not to be outdone by Rick's dress at the summit, here I am "semi-shirtless" standing between the hut and Zealand Falls. Actually, even though the ground was snow covered, the outside temperature was in the fifties.

During the summer months the falls are a popular place for hikers and on warm and sunny days you can see many taking advantage of the cool water. On this day swimming would not be very prudent.

When we arrived at the trail junction we stopped for a photograph; Rick was joined by another hiker accompanied by his friend.

On September 1st we attacked the last three four thousand foot peaks in the Presidential Range: Mts. Eisenhower (4,780'), Pierce (4,310') and Jackson (4,052'). The day started off beautifully; the photograph at the left is Mt. Washington taken from Sugar Hill. We hiked the Edmands Path Trail from the Mt. Clinton Road.

The photograph at right shows me at the trail junction; the ridge from Mt. Franklin and the Crawford Path can be seen behind me.

Mt. Eisenhower Summit – Rick   **Mt. Eisenhower Summit - Me**

The first part of the day was rather pleasant and, on our way between Mt. Jackson and Mt. Pierce, we stopped at the AMC Mizpah Spring Hut (3,800') and enjoyed some chocolate-chip cookies and lemonade. After a brief rest we resumed our hike and struck out for Mt. Pierce. When we reached the summit we still had views; however, the clouds began to roll in and, shortly after taking photographs, the visibility diminished considerably.

We remained on the summit a bit longer than we should have and hiked the last mile or so on the way out on the Webster/Jackson Trail, in the dark. We have since carried headlamps in our knapsacks.

On the 16th of September we attacked Mt. Passaconaway (4,043') and ascended via the Oliverian Brook Trail, Passaconaway Cutoff and the Square Ledge Trail. We left Rick's pack at the intersection of the Cutoff and the Square Ledge Trail; Rick took my pack and we "slackpacked" to the summit. The summit is wooded and has no view but the ledges to the east and north provide excellent views. We encountered our first "snow" in the form of scattered snow showers, however; nothing stuck to the ground.

Returning to the intersection where Rick had left his pack, we rested for a few minutes and had some orange slices and fresh pineapple – just before getting ready to depart, I noticed Rick stuffing my pack into his – he had decided that I should hike the remainder of the trip unencumbered by my pack. As usual, he takes good care of the old man – I can tell you that, although it isn't always necessary, it is always very much appreciated.

Early in the morning on November 18th, we began our next to last hike of the 2011 season up Mt. Galehead (4,024') and, although we had encountered snow and ice at the higher elevations before, this was the first hike that was entirely in those conditions. We stayed together for the first part of the hike and then Rick picked up speed a bit and got ahead of me. I plodded along and for some reason got the idea that I was way behind. When I reached the junction of the Gale River and Garfield Ridge Trails, I had thoughts of turning around and heading back to the parking area. Then I reasoned that since I had gotten this far, I could probably go the distance.– About ten meters from the trail intersection I noticed that Rick had left a message in the snow relative to the time he had departed that point, I looked at my watch and was surprised to find that I was less than fifteen minutes behind him.

When I reached the AMC Galehead Hut I heard Rick yelling for me from the summit – I yelled back at him and told him to wait for me and I would join him in a few minutes.

We stayed at the summit for a while and then descended to the AMC Hut where we rested for a few minutes and had some pineapple chunks that I had brought with me. Refreshed, we headed back down the trail and stopped for some photographs at the junction of the Gale River and Garfield Ridge Trails.

"Lift thine eyes, O lift thine eyes to the mountains, whence cometh help. Thy help cometh from the Lord, the Maker of heaven and earth. He hath said, thy foot shall not be moved, thy Keeper will never slumber.".   Mendelssohn's "Elijah"

A Study of Two Peaks in Two Seasons

Mt. Galehead and the AMC Hut Looking South from North Twin – July 2011

North Twin and the AMC Hut Looking North from Mt. Galehead – November 2011

We started down the Gale River Trail together and after a while Rick picked up his pace again and we parted for a while and then re-united later in the parking area. This hike took place on November 18th, just before Thanksgiving - a day or two later I received this email message from Rick relative to him getting ahead of me on the way back:

Hi Joe……I would like to apologize for not stopping at least two more times on the way out so you could catch up, I was too focused on getting out before dark. My plan was to return back down the trail with flashlights if necessary and without my backpack; however, once again this plan was foiled as the old man teaches the younger man a new lesson and comes strolling out only a few moments behind. It is my wish to be as strong and active as the old boy I am hiking with….it would have been better for me to have stopped and taken a few extra breaks on the out both to rest and enjoy the view…so lesson learned on this hike was take a few extra breaks and enjoy the hike more…my teacher, Dr. Nyberg, has taught this student a lesson even though I was not open to one…now that's a teacher!"

I replied: *"Well Rick, you made my day – God could not have sent me a better hiking companion….I don't mind getting up at 0430 hrs. and driving an hour or so to meet, just the anticipation of the day makes it all worth-while. I look forward to our next adventure and pray that I can keep going for many years to come."*

So the real lesson learned is that hiking, at least for me, is not only to conquer mountain peaks and chalk up mileage but that it creates a medium for the enjoyment of the beauty that God created for us, not only in nature but the beauty of comradery and friendship – I pray that this will continue for many years and don't plan on quitting until I can no longer walk.

Henry David Thoreau wrote:

"I did not wish to take a cabin passage, but rather to go before the mast and on the deck of the world, for there I could best see the moonlight mid the mountains. I do not wish to go below now."

"And now the cold autumnal dews are seen, to cobweb ev'ry green; And by the low-shorn rowens doth appear, the fast declining year." Thoreau

Early on December 2nd Rick and I met on the "Kanc" at the Pine Bend Brook Trail for an excursion to the summit of North Tripyramid (4,180') – it was our last hike of the year. The day was cold but there was no snow. A more detailed description of the trail will be found in Part II when we hiked this trail again to the summit of Middle Tripyramid.

We stopped for photos at the sign indicating the boundary of the Sandwich Range Wilderness:

I didn't take many other photos of this hike except at the summit:

It is now the close of our 2011 hiking season and although we were sad to see it end, we are now filled with excitement and looking forward to the coming season and the completion of the forty-eight peaks.

So we leave you for now, within the shadow of the everlasting hills – may peace be with you this day and until we meet again.

The 2012 Season

"Walk away quietly in any direction and taste the freedom of the mountaineer. Camp out among the grasses and gentians of glacial meadows, in craggy garden nooks full of nature's darlings. Climb the mountains and get their good tidings, Nature's peace will flow into you as sunshine flows into trees. The winds will blow their own freshness into you and the storms their energy, while cares will drop off like autumn leaves. As age comes on, one source of enjoyment after another is closed, but nature's sources never fail."   John Muir

Well, we're now at the first part of May, 2012, and although I did quite a bit of walking in preparation for the upcoming season during February and March while we were at our condominium in West Palm Beach, I recently hit a temporary medical "speed bump." Earlier in April I had outpatient surgery to insert a stent in my right ureter so that the right kidney will drain better. Somehow, complications reared their ugly heads and I ended up with a urinary infection that spun me for a loop. During the last three weeks of April, I spent five days in bed with fever and chills; however, the anti-biotic that I was prescribed did its best and by the end of the month I was near fully recovered. On May 1st I went in again to have the stent removed after which the urologist said the words that I'd been waiting to hear since this ordeal began: "….you may resume ALL your normal activities starting tomorrow…"

Rick got a head start on the season and was able to add Lafayette, Lincoln, Liberty, Flume, Cannon and North Twin to his mountaineering inventory, he still needs quite a few to catch up but he is gaining and I'm anxiously looking forward to our first adventure of the season.

Well that adventure finally took place on the 12th of May. Rick left home at 0200 hrs. and arrived at our home at 0545 hrs. – I was all packed and we transferred his hiking gear to our car and we headed for Gorham, NH and the Carter Moriah Trailhead on Bangor Street.

We hit the trail at 0800 hrs. and I soon realized how out of shape that I was – of course Rick was in shape after his recent hikes in the Franconia region, but I was pitifully slow. The AMC "book" time for the 4.5 mile hike was three hours and fifty-five minutes – we (I) took six hours to reach the summit. There were times when my legs felt like lead and I had trouble getting my "second wind" but I trudged on and the views along the trail were well worth the effort.

The day was glorious, early morning temperatures were in the upper fifties and by the time we had reached the summit the temperature was in the low sixties. The first section of the trail followed an old logging road and passes through areas that were logged many years ago.

After two miles the trail passes a ledge area known as Mt. Surprise (2,194'), that provides beautiful views to the southwest and Mt. Washington (6,288'). A bit later other ledge areas provide excellent views to the southwest and also to the north; one such viewpoint allowed a sweeping view of the town of Gorham (below).

At about 4.2 miles we caught a brief view of the summit and at 4.5 miles we finally saw the sign that pointed to a side trail leading to the actual summit about twenty meters away. The views from the summit were spectacular and unobstructed for three hundred sixty degrees; it was quite windy but that did not take anything away from the enjoyment of being there.

In addition to pleasant views along the trail, Painted Trillium and Purple Trillium flowers were in abundance.

The Painted Trillium (Trillium undulatum) is a member of the Lily Family (Liliaceae) and typically flowers from April through June; its range is from Manitoba to Nova Scotia and Quebec, south to New England and Georgia, and west to Michigan and Wisconsin.

The Purple Trillium (Trillium erectum) is also in the Lily Family with the same flowering months and range as the Painted Trillium above. As with the Painted Trillium, its genus name is taken from the fact that the floral parts and leaves are arranged in threes or multiples of threes.

Rick at the Summit

Me at the Summit

Rick at the Summit Sign **Me at the Summit Sign**

We headed back down the trail at about 1400 hrs. and arrived back at the car just a few minutes after 1900 hrs. We had hiked nine miles in eleven hours, certainly not record time, but I'm hoping for an improvement by the time of our next adventure. For me, thirty-three down, fifteen to go.

On the 17th of May, Rick soloed Mt. Tecumseh (4,003'); I soloed it last July. The trail is rocky and the views from the trail are somewhat limited – part way up the trail there is a short spur that leads to one of the Waterville Valley ski trails and provides views to the north, the most prominent of which is Mt. Osceola and East Osceola. The summit is wooded with limited views.

On the 18th of May, Rick met me at our home at 0500 hrs. and we headed to the small town of Stark, NH for an expedition up Mt. Cabot (4,180'). We began our hike up the Unknown Pond Trail at 0700 hrs.; the temperature was about thirty-five degrees. The day was clear and the forecast was for a high in the low seventies. The first half-mile or so was quite muddy but as we got higher in elevation we lost the mud but acquired no shortage of rocks.

As with our last hike we saw hundreds of Painted Trillium flowers and a few Purple Trilliums, but this time we saw a new wildflower, the Wild Oats; Sessile Bellwort (*Uvularia sessilifolia*). This wildflower is in the Lily Family and has a similar flowering time and range as the Painted and Purple Trillium.

Our first rest stop was at Unknown Pond, at an elevation of about 3,200 feet. There is a campsite there and we had originally planned to camp there overnight and attack the mountain the following day; however, the forecast for the area was for overnight temperatures to be in the mid-thirties which suggested that the overnight temperatures at 3,200 feet near the pond might be in the mid to upper twenties. Based on the forecast we elected to get an early start rather than chance a cold night in a tent.

Unknown Pond

Our next stop was a peak called "The Bulge" (3,950') – it was here that I saw more moose droppings in one spot than I had ever seen in over sixty years of hiking in the New Hampshire woods. Rick got right into the spirit of it and insisted that I take his photo while he inventoried the dozens of piles of droppings in the area. As we continued down the trail we counted another couple of dozen piles in a distance of less than one hundred meters. Although we saw considerable evidence of moose, we did not see any in person.

When we had planned the hike, we had assumed (wrongly) that there was a ridge between The Bulge (3,950') and the summit of Mt. Cabot (4,180'). Unfortunately, we had neglected to check the topographical map as closely as we should have – the trail descended from The Bulge to an elevation of 3,500 feet before it resumed its upward ascent to the summit; so, we descended about five hundred feet before ascending almost seven hundred feet and, of course, we had to do this all over again on our return. The trail was very rocky and the going rather slow; this was the same going up as well as coming down. A short distance south of The Bulge was a 0.3 mile spur to The Horn (3,905') where the views were said to be quite nice; sadly, time did not permit us to take this side trip.

The summit of Mt. Cabot is wooded but there are some views if the hiker is willing to climb a tree or balance precariously on a rock.

Rick at the Summit Sign   **Me at the Summit Sign**

This view was taken from a vantage point a few meters south of the summit; mountains in the Franconia region can be seen in the distance.

The temperature at the summit was about sixty degrees and, although there was a wind, the trees pretty much protected the area from it. We remained at the summit for about forty-five minutes before starting our descent.

The descent was essentially non-eventful but, because he is much faster than I, Rick decided to surge ahead; we agreed to meet at The Bulge, The Horn spur and Unknown Pond. In addition to the rocks already described, there were also hundreds of roots and several blow-downs; one is pictured below.

We rested at Unknown Pond for a short while before heading back to the car. We hiked together for about a mile before Rick sped up; he reached the car about a half hour before I did.

In addition to the wildflowers, there were hundreds of Fiddlehead Ferns along the trail; in the early spring locals frequently harvest them and cook them as vegetables. These plants are said to have antioxidant properties and are a source for Omega 3 and Omega 6; they are also high in iron and fiber.

The Fiddleheads in this photo are just about to unroll into ferns and are inedible at this time. The best time for harvest is in the early spring when the furled fonds are near to the ground and unopened.

Cabot Mountain is #34 on my list of the forty-eight and now I have fourteen remaining; Rick is catching up quite quickly. We will complete the list by mid-summer. One or two of them may require one or two overnights; the remainder can be completed in day trips.

Well, as if hiking Mt. Tecumseh, Cabot Mountain and South Twin weren't enough for a long weekend, Rick decided to push the envelope and hike Mt. Garfield as well – he accomplished all of these in as many days.

Here he is, smiling as usual, at the summit of Garfield; Mt. Lafayette and the Franconia Ridge can be seen over his right shoulder - not a cloud in the sky, an ideal day for a hike.

On May 25th Rick and I agreed to meet at the Sawyer River Road in Crawford Notch to hike Mt. Carrigan (4,700') – we met at 0545 hrs.; to our dismay, the road was still gated. Since we had both hiked this peak before, we decided to go with Plan "B". "Let's try Middle Tripyramid (4,140')." I had made three unsuccessful attempts at this peak but had to turn back because of time constraints; this time I was determined to make it. The weather was not conducive to hiking, however, we parked at the Pine Bend Brook trailhead on the Kancamagus Highway and got started at about 0700 hrs. The first couple of miles were pleasant; however, the trail soon became steeper and rockier and, to make matters worse, about three quarters of the way up it began to pour rain.

The rain caused the rocks and ledges to be quite slippery, reminding us that when we did this trail last winter the rocks were almost as slippery - that time because of ice. By the time we reached the summit of North Tripyramid the rain had stopped but the mist swirled around and at times it looked like smoke.

We put on some dry clothes and headed to Middle Tripyramid (4,140'). Rick had scaled the north peak three times and the middle peak once; I had made the north peak once but had never been successful with my attempts at the middle peak.

The hike between the peaks went well and we arrived back at north peak and took on a little nourishment before heading back down the trail to the car. Because of the slippery conditions the trip down took just about as long, if not longer, as the trip up.

Here is Rick using one of the hundreds of roots that assisted us up some of the steeper ledges. Going down was just as slow as going up – because of the wetness, extreme caution was in order.

And here's Rick again on the "trail" up and down the rock pile that apparently was a brook bed at one time. There is really no trail here; all you do is find the best and safest path from the top to the bottom or vise versa.

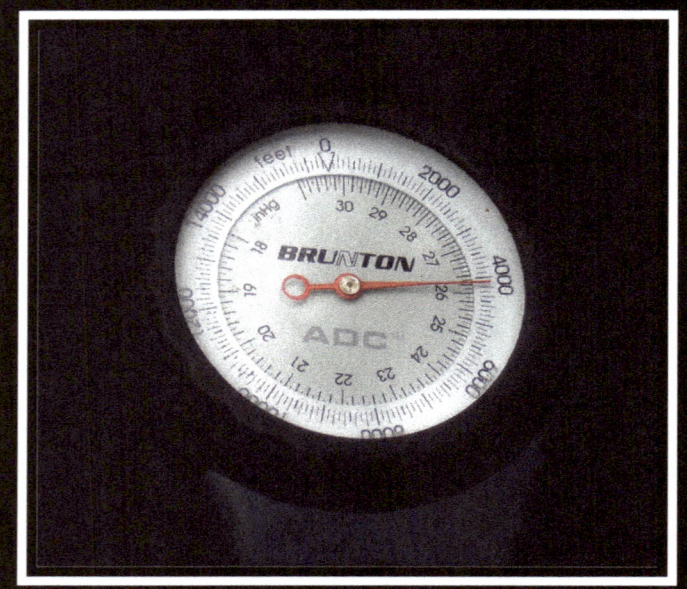

Are we there yet???

The Dynamic Duo at the Summit

Below is a photograph of a small ice cave that we spotted part way down the trail at about the 3,500 foot contour. Ice is not uncommon in the higher elevations even into the summer months.

On the two hikes prior to this one we had identified several types of wildflowers – on this one we saw dozens of Lady's Slippers. Lady's Slippers (Cypripedium acaule) are members of the Orchid Family (Orchidaceae) and generally flower between April and July. The range is from Saskatchewan to Newfoundland and Nova Scotia, south to South Carolina and Georgia, west to Alabama and Tennessee, and north to Minnesota. We observed both white and pink variations of this beautiful wildflower.

Attempts to transplant these fragile flowers are typically unsuccessful and hikers are asked not to pick them.

This hike was peak number thirty-five for me and thirty-two for Rick; we are right on schedule to complete all forty-eight by mid-summer.

June 1st presented itself as an absolutely ideal day for an ambitious hike up Mt. Whiteface (4,020'). Because the trailhead was two hours away, I decided to join Rick at the Grand Hotel in North Conway. Rick had already booked his room and had stayed there the previous night. I was able to get my own room as a "walk-in" and, using the discount card, acquired a nice big room with two queen-sized beds and a large screen TV at a very reasonable price. The hotel had heated indoor and outdoor pools; the latter was only open until 2100 hrs. but the indoor pool remained open quite a while longer. There was also a restaurant and bar so we had all the comforts of home.

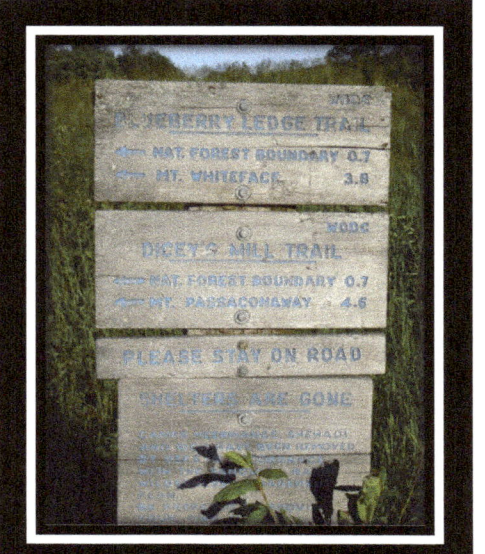

After a relaxing evening we drove to the Wonalancet P.O. and were on the Blueberry Ridge Trail at 0600 hrs.

The Blueberry Ridge Trail is probably the most popular trail for the ascent and was laid out by Gordon Taylor and opened in 1899. The first part of the trail is a road that follows the stream before crossing on "Squirrel Bridge." Once the bridge is crossed the road turns sharply to the right and soon joins the trail.

The first three miles took us along the brook and through forests of pine and mixed hardwoods. At two miles we encountered large areas of rock ledge but the going was relatively easy. The photos below were taken at the intersection of the Blueberry Ledge Trail and the Blueberry Ledge Cutoff on the lower ledges – this intersection is at the two mile mark. The views at this spot were limited.

From this point on, the trail ascended moderately and took us through the same type of forest; the trail was well maintained and well-marked. At some spots the trail crews had actually constructed small rock stairways; there were several of these along the next mile or so.

The majority of this hike was in the Sandwich Range Wilderness and this trail was maintained by the Wonalancet Out Door Club; they do a superb job at trail maintenance.

We continued on the trail and at the 3.6 mile point we came across the first of the steep ledges that had to be crossed before reaching the summit. The AMC White Mountain Guide describes the upper trail in part as follows: "...*where it abruptly approaches the edge of a steep cliff and may be dangerous if slippery.*"

The guidebook continues: *"Just beyond here, it climbs a steep ledge, then continues to scramble up the steep, rough, rocky ridge with several excellent viewpoints, ending at the ledges of the lower south summit."*

The photo at left shows the drill holes that were made to support wooden steps that were installed to assist hikers in negotiating this set of rock ledges. The steps have been removed and the remaining holes do little to assist the hiker in negotiating these sets of ledges.

There were some helpful roots and trees along the ledges but for the most part, handholds and footholds in the rocks had to be found.

In the photo at right I am using two rock outcroppings as handholds while I attempt to step up with my left foot. Once that foot is in place I can get my right foot sideways just below that dark area below my right hand. I can then boost my body flat on the area where my right hand is and look for another set of handholds. It looks easier than it is and suppose that if I were fifty years younger, this would be a breeze.

The photo at right shows me "negotiating" this ledge on our way down. Note that here I was pleased that God gave me a posterior that allowed me to slide a somewhat controlled descent to the base of the ledge. A branch served to provide some support before the descent began.

Looking South

We finally reached the south summit and the views from here were spectacular; we stayed here for a few minutes and took photos before heading for the "true summit" about 0.2 miles distant.

Lake Winnipesaukee in the distance, Squam Lake at far right.

Rick Standing on the brink of Eternity

Looking East – Mt. Chocorua in the Distance

Looking Northeasterly – Mt. Washington in the Distance

The hike from the south summit to the "true summit" was pretty uneventful and the summit was rather lackluster. Had there not been a cairn there to mark the spot we would have hiked right by it; the site was completely wooded with no views whatsoever. Here's Rick posing at the summit cairn.

I had Rick take a photo of me at the summit just to prove that I made it as well. This is peak number thirty-six for me and I have twelve remaining.

It was a challenging day but it was fully enjoyable and rewarding. The forecast for this coming week is rain almost every day so it might be more than a week before we begin another adventure – no matter when we get a chance to go again, we both look forward to it with excitement.

Mt. Whiteface from Ferncroft

After a stretch of meteorological inclemencies, June 11th presented itself as a suitable day for a hike. Rick called and asked if I would join him on a hike to Mt. Monroe (5,372'); I had scaled this peak in 1965 but since I hadn't hiked in over a week I agreed.

The Higher Summits Forecast published by the Mount Washington Observatory read as follows:

"In the clear under partly sunny skies, Highs in the mid 50's and wind W shifting to SW 15-30 mph decreasing to 5-20 mph."

An ideal day for a hike (sadly, it was also an ideal day for black flies). So we met at the Ammonoosuc Ravine Trail trailhead at 0700 hrs. and began our adventure. The first 2.1 miles is pretty straightforward and, for the most part, follows the banks of the Ammonoosuc River in generally easy grades. At 2.1 miles the trail crosses the outlet of Gem Pool, a beautiful pool at the foot of a cascade.

The water was crystal clear and cold and the numerous cascades along the entire trail were indeed a pleasant sight.

At this point the trail got increasingly steeper and rougher; at 2.3 miles there was a side-path to a viewpoint at the junction of two beautiful waterslides that end in a pool at the foot of the gorge.

"Within these plantations of God, a decorum of sanctity reigns." Emerson

Above this point the main portion of the brook falls down six hundred feet in a steep trough in the mountainside.

The trail continues rather roughly and steeply with several minor brook crossings until it reaches an area where the ledges become more frequent. There are many viewpoints along the ledge area, mostly to the northwest. The ledges are steep and difficult to navigate; in wet weather it would be prudent to avoid them.

At about 3.0 miles the trail leaves the scrub pines at the treeline and at 3.1 reaches the location of the AMC Lakes of the Clouds Hut (5,012'). The Lakes of the Clouds Hut is one of eight huts operated by the AMC and is located on the southern shoulder of Mt. Washington on the ridge between it and Mt. Monroe. The hut accommodates ninety hikers and forty-three were scheduled for that night.

Lake of the Clouds is a spring fed mountain lake and the source for the Ammonoosuc River. Ammonoosuc is the Abnaki word for *small, narrow fishing place.* The river is fifty-five miles in length and flows through several NH towns including my hometown of Lisbon.

As legend has it, back in July 1820, Ethan Allen Crawford and Phillip Carrigan had led a group of hikers up to the summit of Mount Washington. As the story goes, on their descent they came across a pond which they named Blue Pond; that pond is now known as Lake of the Clouds.

Is it really that high up? **Yuuup!**

The summit of Mt. Monroe is about a ten or fifteen minute hike from the hut. Rick made the ascent but, since I had scaled the summit before, I elected to stay at the hut and eat my lunch. The summit of Mt. Monroe was clear but the summit of adjacent Mt. Washington was in and out of the clouds most of the day.

Mt. Monroe **Mt. Washington**

We departed the summit at about 1315 hrs. and although the hike down took less time than the hike up, the ledges presented an equal challenge during the descent. We met several groups of hikers on our way down, one couple was from Canada and I greeted them with my best French, ***Bonjour - vous êtes du Canada ?*** They responded that they were Canadians but did not speak French – bummer!

Here is Rick negotiating one of the more difficult brook crossings on the way down.

Make sure to keep a firm grip on the handrail Rick!

It was a tiring and somewhat strenuous hike, but all-in-all it was a very enjoyable day. We have yet to plan our next adventure but whatever it is we're hoping for hikeable weather next week.

Well, hikeable weather finally appeared on July 5th. I arose at 0400 hrs., dressed and put my thirty some odd pound pack in the car and at 0445 hrs. and headed to the Zealand Trail trailhead to meet Rick.

At 0551 hrs. we were on the trail – the plan was to hike Zealand Mountain (4,260'), Mt. Guyot (4,580'), West Bond (4,540'), Mt. Bond (4,698') and Bondcliff (4,265'). We were hoping to add Owl's Head (4,025') to the expedition but that didn't work out.

Our first rest stop was the AMC Zealand Falls Hut after which Rick picked up his pace and waited for me at Zeacliff. We parted again and I didn't see him again until I reached the summit of Mt. Guyot. The day was cool and damp and the forecast was for the upper peaks to be in the clouds with a possibility of rain showers – unfortunately, the possibility of rain showers turned into a fact and it rained for a couple of hours. The photograph is of me at the summit of Zealand Mountain where I arrived at the same time as another hiker – I offered to take his photo if he would do the same for me; he told me that it was the first time anyone had offered. The Zealand summit is quite "lackluster" in that it is completely wooded with no view whatsoever.

When I arrived at the signpost that announced the Zealand Spur Trail 0.1 mile, there was a note attached to the sign that read: *"Hello Dr. Joe – I left here at 11:00 a.m. Richard ps. Going to set up camp! Will return down trail to you ASAP."*

I put on my pack and headed up the trail for Mt. Guyot and met Rick just a short distance from the summit. The summit, with the exception of small pines, is essentially bare but since it was completely enshrouded by clouds, there was no view. Fortunately the rain had ceased.

Me at the Summit of Mt. Guyot

Rick at the Summit Checking His Cellphone

Much of the trail is rocky and for me, who will reach age seventy-six in two months, slow going.

It's probably not amazing that fifty years ago I would have made "book time" or better on these trails but experience seems to come with age and possibly better judgment – my judgment told me to take it slow; to date I have never had a serious accident and my inner voice tells me to take time, be careful and arrive home safely.

I intend to do just that!

More caution and even slower going, at least for me, is the negotiation of rock ledges such as the one pictured at left. This one is between twelve and fourteen feet in height and was encountered on descent – the official term for negotiating rock ledges such as these is referred to as "scrambling." I tend to call it……………well, never mind.

Then every once in a while, some kind souls make things just a tad easier.

Page 79

From Mt. Guyot we continued along the Twinway and in a short time reached the junction of the Twinway and the Bondcliff Trails. The campsite was a mile away; although Rick had already been there, gotten a tent platform and registered. He did not set up the tent deciding to wait until I arrived before doing so, because he had not set up this particular one before.

The tent is a three man tent and is quite roomy for two – set-up takes about ten minutes or so. The campsite is run by the AMC and offers tent platforms and a cabin; there is a spring, dishwashing area, and toilet facility. The entrance trail to the campsite is rocky and about 0.2 miles in length.

When Rick had arrived, there was only a group of four that had gotten there before him; later more hikers arrived and by nightfall the area was well occupied.

While we were paying for our stay, the campsite director told us that he was planning to hike West Bond that evening to watch the sunset – after discussing it for a bit, I decided to join Rick, and check it out since we had to hike West Bond anyway. Sunset was about 1930 hrs. and because the round trip was about a mile and a half, we struck out at 1830 hrs.

We arrived at the summit just about when we had anticipated that we would but, since the peak was still in the clouds with no view whatsoever, we thought it prudent not to descend a rather steep and ledgey approach in the dark; we took a couple of photographs and headed back to the campsite.

The pack that I carried was the same one that I had used fifty years ago when I was hiking and camping on a regular basis; the compact cook-stove was also that old and was made in Sweden for backpacking purposes. Although I hadn't used the stove in a long time, it worked perfectly.

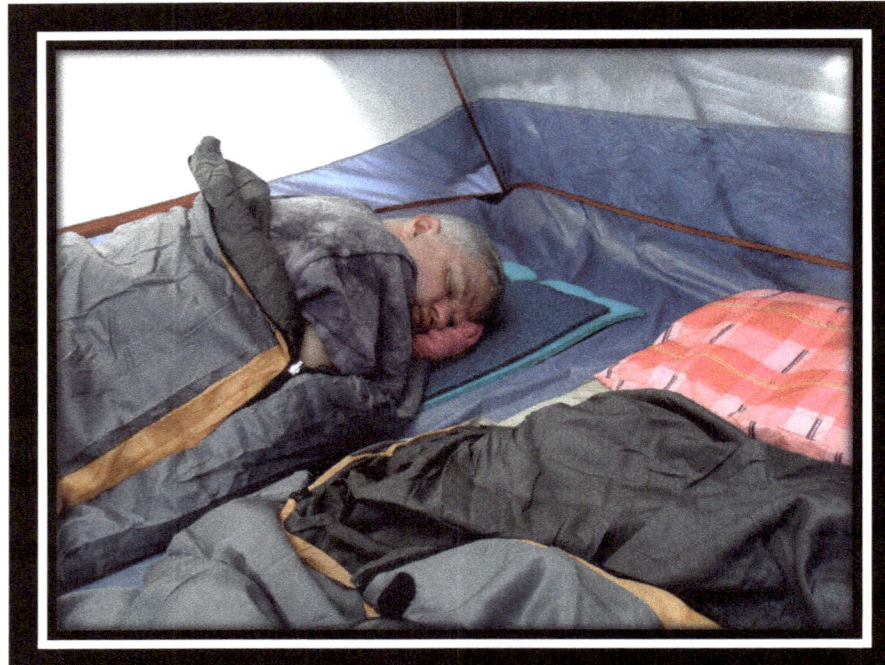

Rick had complained about our neighbors talking loudly and that he was unable to sleep.

I will reserve comment and let the readers decide for themselves.

The following day we broke camp and headed for the Bondcliff Trail and Mts. Bond and Bondcliff. Again Rick picked up his pace and arrived at the summit of Mt. Bond about fifteen or twenty minutes ahead of me.

We posed for a photograph at the summit; incidentally, this is the only photograph to date that shows both of us together. Bondcliff, 1.2 miles away, is at the right side of the photograph.

From the summit we had gorgeous views:

Mt. Guyot,

Mts. Garfield, Galehead, South Twin, West Bond.

Owl's Head in the foreground and the Franconia Ridge in the distance.

The trail to Bondcliff was rocky and slow going for me; Rick reached the summit long before I did.

This is the final approach to the summit – slightly left and below of center you can see a rock cairn. These cairns are typically found above the tree line and are strategically placed for roped parties to move from one to the other in inclement weather.

The lead hiker will head out to find the next cairn and then signal the rest to proceed. It is a lifesaver but it ain't necessarily fun.

Here is Rick again standing on the brink of eternity. This is one of the most popular photo spots, just below the summit - the drop is about two thousand feet below.

I was just a tad more cautious and decided to stand a few feet back from the edge of eternity.

From the summit, the trail wound its way 4.4 miles to meet the Wilderness Trail, formerly the railroad bed of the East Branch logging railroad that served the area from 1893 to 1948. The Lincoln East Branch logging railroad was the largest in New England and its tracks totaled seventy-two miles. The southern terminus of the Bondcliff Trail is the site of the old railroad Camp 16.

Map of the East Branch and Lincoln Railroad System

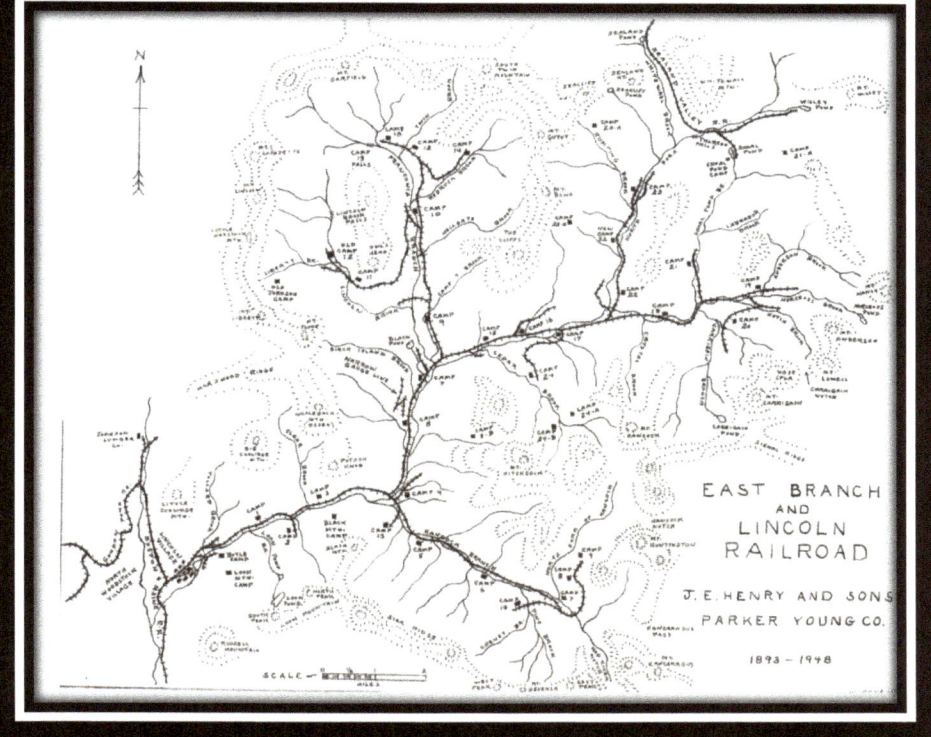

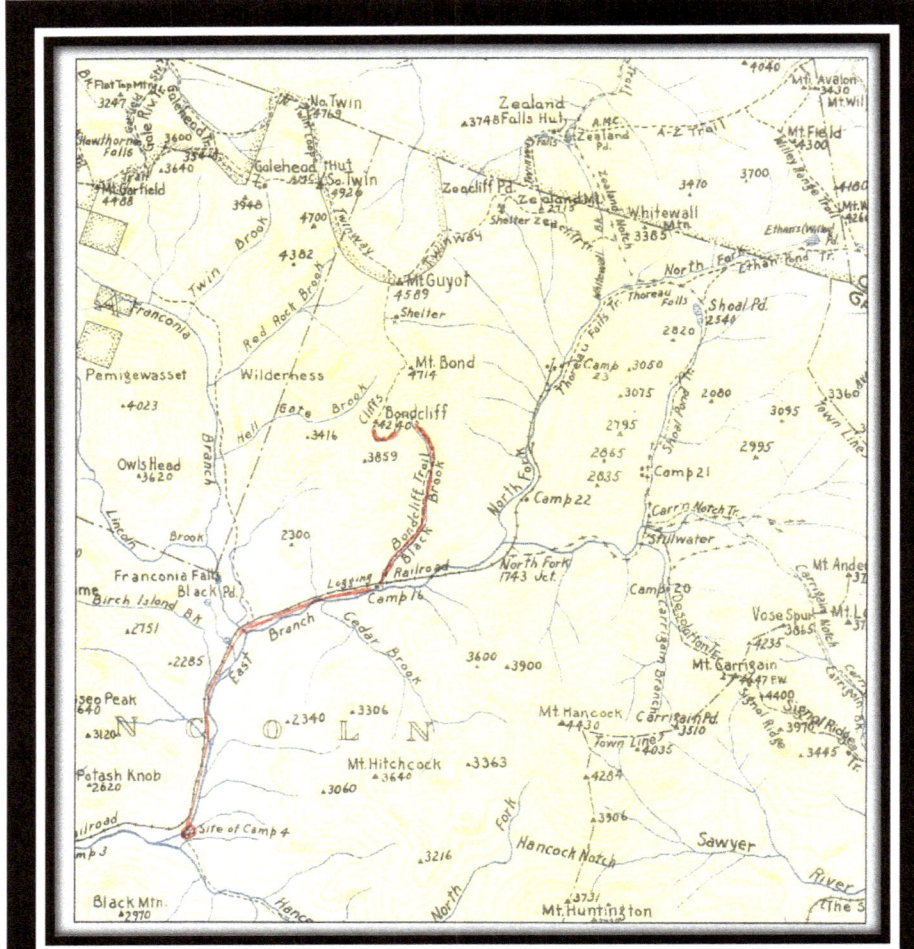

This 1934 AMC Trail Map shows our route from Bondcliff to the Wilderness and Lincoln Woods Trails. Note that the Bondcliff Trail ends at the site of old railroad Camp 16 and the Lincoln Woods Trail ends at the site of Camp 4, now the parking area for the USFS Lincoln Woods Visitor Center. The route, marked in red, is nine miles long.

When we were re-united later, Rick said that he had waited for me at the end of the Bondcliff Trail for about an hour before moving along. The time was about 1700 hrs. when I arrived and since he wasn't there I guessed that he was concerned that it would be dark before we reached the Lincoln Woods parking area and decided to move along.

The portion of the Wilderness Trail between the Bondcliff and Lincoln Woods Trail is 1.8 miles and because it is almost level I made the trek in just over an hour. When I reached the junction I spotted a note that Rick had left with the time – I was less than ten minutes behind at that point.

I crossed the Franconia Brook and rested for a few minutes before walking the last two and a half miles to the parking area. Rick's note said that his plan was to go ahead and call my wife Dawn and then come back with flashlights to meet me. To his surprise, I arrived at the parking area shortly after his arrival, no flashlights necessary – we both waited for Dawn to come and pick us up.

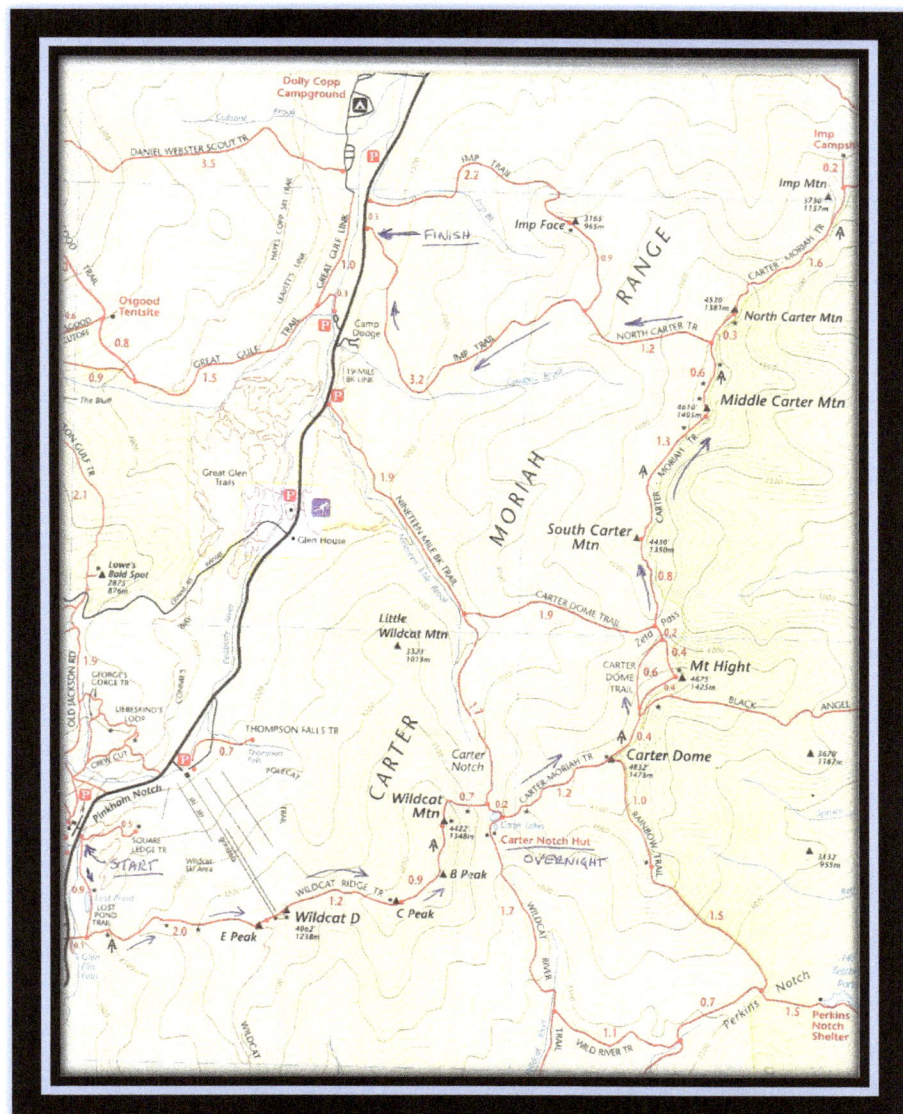

July 19th and 20th were forecast to be ideal days for a hike, so we decided to attack the two Wildcats and the three Carters. We started our adventure from the Pinkham Notch AMC Visitor Center at 0700 hrs. on Thursday. The plan was to hike the Wildcat Ridge Trail, overnight at the AMC Carter Notch Hut and continue on to the Carters the following day. The Wildcat Ridge Trail actually crosses five four thousand foot peaks but only two of them count toward the Four Thousand Foot Club.

The Wildcat Ridge Trail was one of the most steep and difficult trails that I recall hiking during my sixty plus years in the White Mountains. The distance from the AMC Center to the Carter Notch Hut is six miles; it took me twelve hours to cover this distance.

Sadly, none of the five peaks is identified, although "D" peak has an observation deck built on the summit and "A" peak is within a couple of feet of a viewpoint that looks over Carter Notch, those are kind of no brainers; however, we could only guess the location of the rest of them.

View of the Wildcats and Carters from Glen Boulder

Another view from Glen Boulder looking east, the Wildcat Trail pretty much follows the ridge in the center of the photo. Wildcat "D" is slightly right of center; just below the summit you can make out the top of the Wildcat Mountain Ski Lift. There are actually five four thousand foot peaks in the Wildcats, A Peak (4,422'), B Peak (4,330'), C Peak (4,298'), D Peak (4,062'), and E Peak (4,046'); unfortunately only Wildcat A and Wildcat D are recognized because of the two hundred foot "prominence" requirement. Essentially, this rule states that a hiker must descend a minimum of 200 feet before climbing to reach a higher peak.

As noted earlier, we left the AMC Visitor Center parking area and crossed the highway to the Lost Pond Trail, this was to avoid crossing the Ellis River which was said to be high.

The Lost Pond Trail added another mile to our hike and although rocky, it was fairly level and we made the Wildcat Ridge Trail junction in just about a half hour.

The photograph at left is Rick at the Wildcat Ridge and Lost Pond Trail junction sign.

We found later that the river crossing would have been relatively easy that day – well, it's better to be safe than sorry.

The day was glorious and the visibility was over one hundred miles. Part way up the trail we met a 22 year old young lady who was planning to hike the entire Appalachian Trail, her name is Charlotte and her trail name "Booterman". All through trail hikers all have a "trail name" of some sorts. She got her name by rescuing a hiker's boot during a river crossing. It seems that when the two reached the river they took off their boots in order to wade across – Charlotte had evidently been successful at tossing her boots to the far shore; the other hiker was not quite as fortunate and her boot began to float downstream. Charlotte was just able to save the boot with her trekking pole and acquired the trail name.

We met many other hikers during our hike but none quite as attractive and friendly as Charlotte. Friendliness is the key along with a willingness to help – strange in a way, but I wonder why the same philosophy is not enjoyed in everyday living off trail.

We've met many "through hikers" (those that are hiking the entire Appalachian Trail from Maine to Georgia), others are day hikers, some hike from one AMC Hut to another, some overnight in tents or in the open, others have a goal of completing the four thousand footers in NH or in New England, and many simply are out enjoying nature and what God has created for us to enjoy. Simple love of the outdoors is the only motivation for them – actually, I believe that all of us, even those with various other motives, are motivated by the love of the outdoors.

The Wildcat Ridge Trail gave us plenty of opportunity to "scramble" up the many ledges that we had to maneuver during our hike. Here is Rick near the top of one of them.

Naturally, if Rick had to scramble up, you know who had to do the same thing.

I don't remember what I was doing in this photograph, but it appears that I am praying for Divine guidance.

It must have worked because I'm almost at the top of this ledge.

The view of Mt. Washington (6,288') from a viewpoint (3,500') about one-half miles from "E" peak was absolutely spectacular. The summit is in the center of the photograph with the Huntington Ravine to the right and the Tuckerman Ravine to the left. The trail from Boot Spur can be seen to the left of Tuckerman's.

We finally arrived at the observation deck on Wildcat "D" (4,062') just in time for a break and a brief nap. Here is Rick taking full advantage of the rest stop.

From here Rick charged on ahead and I didn't see him again until I was near the junction of the Wildcat Ridge Trail and the Nineteen Mile Brook Trail. He did leave a note with his time of departure from Wildcat Mountain (4,422') along with his watch – at this point I was about forty minutes behind him. There was a viewpoint there that overlooked the Carter Notch and provided a good look at the AMC Hut 1,000 feet below; it was here that we planned to spend the night.

I have hiked New Hampshire and the White Mountains for over sixty years and had never stayed in an AMC Hut before. I have visited several and had enjoyed lemonade and cookies there but have never spent a night, so this was going to be a first. But - I had to get there first and had a mile to hike and a thousand feet to descend before my arrival. The trail was steep and rocky but that's really nothing new in the White Mountains. About two-thirds of the way down there was a rockslide and a very nice view to the north – I stopped and called my wife Dawn on the cell phone to let her know that I was still alive; while I was on the phone Rick arrived to let me know that, although I would arrive at the hut after dinnertime, they would hold dinner for me. He had already checked-in and let the crew know that I would not be too far behind.

The AMC has a system of huts that accommodate hikers with sleeping quarters, dinner, and breakfast. They are generally spaced so that you can hike from one to another without packing food or overnight bedding, although it is wise to carry a sleeping bag.

Here is a photograph of the entrance to the hut – you can see the Wildcat peak, one thousand feet above our location, in the upper center of the photo.

This night only nine people were in residence so we all had rooms to ourselves; Rick and I shared a room with four bunks, two lowers and two uppers. Mattresses, blankets and a pillow were provided – the facility was clean and the food was quite nicely prepared.

During dinner I jokingly asked for a wine list – the hutmaster remarked that he wished he had one, but….. Anyway, one of the hikers at the dinner table disappeared and came back with a bottle of Pinot Noir – not only did he have one but he was actually willing to share! A pleasant surprise indeed.

Here I am with the hut crew right after breakfast and just before we ventured out for the Carters.

The crew members were very friendly and courteous; it was a pleasurable experience for my first night in a hut – I couldn't have lost my AMC hut virginity to a better crew.

We got started for the last segment of our trip at 0800 hrs. and, after passing the Carter Lakes, headed up the Carter-Moriah Trail. This trail begins at the shore of the larger lake and crosses Carter Dome, Mt. Hight, South Carter, Middle Carter, North Carter, Imp Mountain, and Mt. Moriah before terminating in the town of Gorham, NH. The entire trail is 13.8 mile; however, since North Carter Mountain did not count toward our goal and since we had already hiked Mt. Moriah earlier in the season, we elected to go only as far as the North Carter and Imp Trails.

This is a photograph of the larger of the two Carter Lakes; the Carter-Moriah Trail is just a short distance from where this photograph was taken.

The elevation here is about 3,200 feet so we had to hike 1.2 miles with a gain in elevation of just over 1,600 feet; the elevation of Carter Dome is 4,832 feet.

There was a very pleasant viewpoint a short way up the trail that gave me the opportunity for another photograph of the hut and the smaller of the two lakes.

The elevation at this point is about four thousand feet, or some eight hundred feet above the hut.

The trail from the lake to the summit of Carter Dome was steep and very rocky, as usual Rick got to the summit before me. The summit is mostly wooded but there were some pleasant views to the north. At one time there was a fire tower there, but only the supports remain; the true summit is marked by a stone cairn, centered on the site of the former fire tower.

Rick at the Summit of Carter Dome **Me at the summit of Carter Dome**

We continued on our way and, although Mt. Hight was reported to afford gorgeous views to the east, we were concerned about time and elected bypassing it instead using the Carter Dome Trail. Although the AMC Guidebook noted that there was a sign at the summit of South Carter (4,430'), our next target, we were unable to find any evidence that we were actually on the summit, although it was pretty obvious that we were.

Our next and last peak was Middle Carter (4,610') – the Guidebook also stated that this peak was marked – well, OK; someone had taken a magic marker and written the name and elevation on a dead tree sticking out behind the summit cairn.

Me at the summit of Middle Carter

Rick at the summit of Middle Carter
After I took this photo, Rick shook hands with me and said: "Only two more to go!"

From Middle Carter we proceeded over a couple of more humps before arriving at the junction of the Carter-Moriah and North Carter Trails – the map indicated that it was only 0.6 miles but it seemed more, perhaps because we were starting to tire a bit.

Well; if I thought that the 0.6 miles was long, the next segment was 1.2 miles – it seemed to take forever, now I know why New Hampshire is called the Granite State. Rick left a note at the point where the Imp Trail intersects with the North Carter Trail – he was about a half hour ahead of me, I was having my usual difficulty with the rocky trail – I had 3.2 miles left before reaching the parking area and recalled that the Guidebook alleged that the lower portion of the trail had been a logging road "meandering" through the forest. Nothing could have been further from the truth – perhaps during the winter months a log skidder may have made its way up part of the trail, but a logging road? No way.

I came to a large white birch blowdown across the trail and saw that Rick had left a rather crude note for me on the backside of a piece of birchbark. It read the time that he had passed and also gave me an indication that he was having as much trouble with the trail as I was.

It was getting late and I had some concern about the remaining daylight but was still confident that I could make it out before dark – I was carrying lights. About ten minutes before reaching the trailhead, Rick showed up and we hiked out together – I had hiked ten miles in about eleven hours.

When I got in Rick's truck, he turned to me and said: ***"There are a lot of 76 year olds in bed right now wishing that they could do what you just did."*** I took that as a compliment and as we drove back to the AMC Visitor Center we discussed what we would do in our next adventure – right now it looks like either Owl's Head in the Pemigewasset Wilderness or Mt. Isolation.

Well, it turned out that August 7th was forecasted to be a spectacular day for hiking and because Mt. Isolation (4,003') had much better view potential than Owl's Head, we decided to attack Mt. Isolation.

The week before we made a "practice run" up the Glen Boulder Trail to determine if the best route would be via that trail for the hike up with the return via the Davis Path, Isolation and Rocky Branch Trails. After scaling the ledges up to the Glen Boulder, I decided that even though the route via the Rocky Branch, Isolation and Davis Path was longer, I really didn't want to hike up to Glen Boulder again.

So, I got up at 0400 hrs. and proceeded to Pinkham Notch and met Rick at the trailhead at 0600 hrs., twenty minutes later we were on our way up the Rocky Branch Trail.

The early part of the trail rose moderately to a "height of land" and then descended to the first Rocky Branch brook crossing where it met the Isolation Trail.

The trail followed the Rocky Branch and we experienced three more crossings. Both trails were rocky, wet and, in many cases, mucky. After the last crossing the trail proceeded north before turning west to meet the Davis Path.

The distance from the Davis Path junction to the Mt. Isolation spur path was 0.9 miles; up until this point I was able to make about a mile an hour – the last 0.9 went a little faster.

It took me eight hours to cover the seven miles to the summit but it was well worth the effort, the views were 360 degrees The clouds were few and widely scattered. The visibility was virtually unlimited and the wind was less than ten knots.

Me at the Summit Cairn   **Rick at the Summit Cairn**

We spent about twenty minutes at the summit before heading back down; at this point we were concerned about time and running out of daylight – we had headlamps but were hoping that we wouldn't have to use them.

We made our way back to the Davis Path where Rick posed for a photo by the Isolation Spur sign – we made the 0.9 mile back to the Isolation Trail junction in twenty-five minutes so it appeared that our trip back to the trailhead would go a little faster than the trip up.

In fact, the trip down did go a bit faster but managing the rocky trail for me was still problematic.

On the way up, at the first brook crossing, we had decided that when we came back we would stop and take a brief session in the water so that we could refresh ourselves for the final four miles to the parking area. We knew that we were pushing the daylight envelope but were determined to make the stop. We arrived at the crossing at 1700 hrs. and estimated that we could make the last leg in three hours, so we had to be out of the water, dried, dressed and ready to go no later than 1730 hrs. This would put us back to our vehicles at dark.

Here's Rick getting ready to make the plunge.

Here I am making an attempt to brush the icicles off my body after I made the plunge. OK, no icicles, but the water was quite cool.

We were dressed and ready to go and at 1730 hrs. headed back down the trail. Shortly after passing the boundary marker for the Presidential Wilderness, Rick surged ahead. Since I have hiked with him many times, I knew that his plan was to get to the parking area first, drop off his pack and return with flashlights to "rescue" me.

Well, I really didn't need to be rescued because I arrived at the trailhead at 2018 hrs. and met Rick just as he was walking across the parking lot to come back on the trail. I was able to make it back without the need for artificial light. The return trip took me six hours.

It was a long day, fourteen miles in fourteen hours – the longest mileage in a single day since we had begun to hike with each other. The day was a very pleasant one and Mt.Isolation was number forty-seven – one to go! Owl's Head will be the last – the hike to this one is eighteen miles round trip so I'll have to rest up for that adventure. An overnight might be an option.

WE MADE IT!!!

The August 14th High Peaks Forecast from the Mt. Washington Observatory looked favorable for a trip to Owl's Head (4,025') and our final hike in pursuit of the elusive New Hampshire four thousand footers.

I spoke with Rick on the telephone and we decided to sleep in the cars so we could get on the trail early in the morning. However, when I called him back to confirm he advised me that he had reserved a suite in one of the Lincoln resort hotels – OK: hot tub, pool, Jacuzzi in the bedroom and all the amenities – and we would be less than five miles from the trailhead! The best part was that I could have my wife Dawn join me that evening. We liked the rooms so well that we decided to stay an extra night – what a way to end a full day of hiking; a nice hot shower and a glass or two or three of wine.

I set the alarm for 0400 hrs. on Tuesday and we were at the Lincoln Woods Visitor Center parking area at 0430 hrs. and on the trail twenty minutes later. We put on our headlamps and crossed the suspension bridge over the East Branch before setting out on the Lincoln Woods Trail. This trail was formerly the Wilderness Trail but the name was changed by the forestry service because the first 2.9 miles of the trail was outside of the Pemigewasset Wilderness.

Many of the trails we followed that day were former logging railroad beds, accordingly; we made the first 2.9 miles in just under an hour and rested for a few moments at the stone RR bridge abutment before heading across the river to join the Franconia Brook Trail. This was our last easy river/brook crossing – the photo at left was taken just about fifteen minutes after sunrise.

The next segment was along the Franconia Brook Trail; this portion of the hike was 1.7 miles and we made that in just over one half hour. At the 1.7 mile mark we paused for a couple of minutes to take photographs at the junction of the Franconia Brook and Lincoln Brook Trails. At this point the Lincoln Brook Trail turns in a general westerly direction before reaching our first unbridged brook crossing over Franconia Brook.

Rick at the trail junction **Me at the trail junction**

In about one-half mile we arrived at the Franconia Brook crossing. A brief word about these brook crossings is in order here. The AMC White Mountain Guide, 28th Edition, describes the brook crossings as follows: *"These crossings, which are not easy even in moderate water levels and are particularly difficult at high water……"*

In anticipation of high water Rick wore sneakers and I wore low leather moccasins to facilitate the crossings in the event that we were not able to "rock hop" our way across – hiking boots would be put on later for the climb up Owl's Head "herd path".

The dynamic duo at the first brook crossing

We negotiated this crossing without incident and then came across the second in another half mile. This one was a little more challenging.

We had a few more crossings before the last one – here Rick is demonstrating his best brook crossing technique. Because we were about a quarter mile from the Owl's Head Trail, it was here that we dried our feet, changed socks and put on our hiking boots.

The Owl's Head "Trail" is an unofficial, unmarked path that follows a rock slide 1.1 miles from the junction of the Lincoln Brook Trail to the summit. The change in elevation is about fifteen hundred feet in that distance and great care had to be taken to avoid a serious accident.

Because the trail is not maintained, the USFS does not allow any trail signs or markings; however, some thoughtful hikers have made up some rather unique signs of their own.

In over sixty years of hiking the White Mountains of New Hampshire, I'm of the opinion that this is another of the most difficult trails that I've encountered to date.

The better part of the trail was steep and consisted mainly of loose rocks, most of which were dry; however, there were several sections that were wet with spring runoffs and very slippery. Where there were no ledges or rocks, the trail was muddy.

The 1.1 mile climb up took us over two hours; it was even longer going down.

Part way up the slide there was a very pleasant view to the west and the Franconia Ridge that stretches from Mt. Lafayette to Mt. Flume.

Owl's Head has two "summits", The first is now referred to as the "false" summit and for years it was assumed to be the "true" summit; however, at some point in time hikers using GPS equipment and other electronic gear capable of determining elevation discovered the "true" summit about 0.2 miles away from the so-called "false" summit.

There is no single trail directly connecting the "summits" – instead, there is a rather frustrating spider-web network of bushwhacking trails, some or possibly all of which eventually lead the hiker to the official summit.

After a few futile attempts we finally found it and fortunately there was a fellow hiker there that agreed to take our photograph.

Well, as previously mentioned, the trip down the slide took more time than the climb up – now we were beginning to be concerned about the hike out. We had headlamps but really didn't look forward to brook crossings in the dark. Nonetheless, we had to make sure that we were more than careful going down the slide.

Although Rick is much faster on the trail, his time down was pretty consistent with mine.

We did make it down without incident and started the hike back to the parking area. At the last brook crossing Rick heard the water calling to him: "Riiiiicccckky, Riiiickkky, come in, come in, commmmme-onnnn in……………." so……

Although I had joined him for a short but refreshing dip in the Rocky Branch during our last hike to Mt. Isolation, somehow I didn't hear the same voices he did, so I decided that, although tempted, I chose not join him this time.

From that point on we made very good time and reached the bridge about one-half hour before sunset.

We rested here for about ten minutes, put on our headlamps and hiked the last two of the 2.9 miles to the parking area in the dark. As we crossed the suspension bridge across the East Branch it began to rain. Rain had threatened all day and we even had a few drops as we descended the rock slide – but, fortunately, it held off until we were within the USFS Visitor Center parking area and on our way back to the hotel.

When we returned to our suite at the resort hotel, my wife Dawn came out to meet me and back in the room I found a cold bottle of champagne waiting for us (compliments of my in-laws), a bottle of wine, cards, certificates of achievement and a balloon (compliments of my wife).

This has been an adventure that many thought was impossible for someone my age – that was all I needed to hear and I pushed myself to the limit because I believed that I could do it, and, with God's unfailing help and the support of Rick and Dawn, I did!

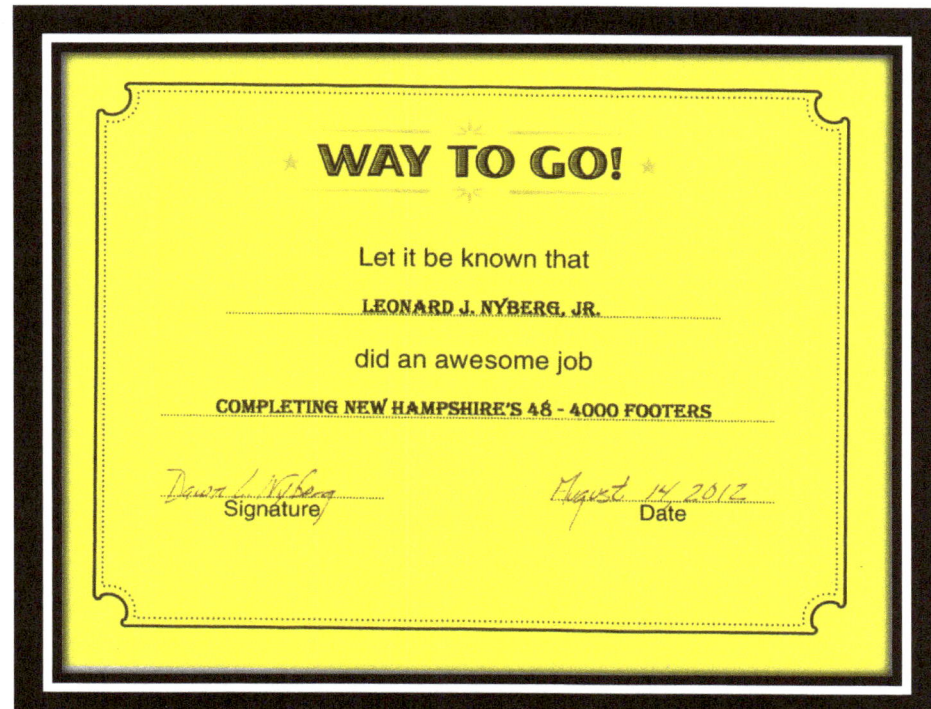

Here is the certificate that Dawn created for me; she made one for Rick also.

What a great experience! Although it took me almost sixty years to complete all forty-eight, the last two years were probably the most enjoyable because I had a purpose and, as it turned out, Rick finally had acquired a purpose as well.

"When a distinguished but elderly scientist states that something is possible, he is almost certainly right. When he states that something is impossible, he is very probably wrong."

Arthur C. Clarke's 1st Law

THE ONLY WAY TO DISCOVER THE LIMITS OF THE POSSIBLE, IS TO VENTURE A LITTLE WAY BEYOND THEM INTO THE IMPOSSIBLE.

Arthur C. Clarke's 2nd Law

Well, we finished the forty-eight peaks in New Hampshire that were in excess of four thousand feet and that made us eligible for membership in the AMC Four Thousand Footer Club.

I filled out an application for both Rick and I and submitted it with this record of our achievements (next page), I also sent a self-addressed and stamped envelope for the return of this book; however, when the letter of acceptance came there was a request to keep the book – of course, I complied.

OK, now we were official members of the AMC Four Thousand Footer Club, in which there are several categories of membership: all in one season, all in the winter, all in order of elevation, etc. In addition there is another certificate for New England's Four Thousand Footers; this includes peaks in Maine and Vermont in addition to the peaks in New Hampshire. There are sixty-seven peaks in all, at present we have fifty-two so our work is cut out for us in 2013. After that? Well, there is New England's One Hundred Highest – oh, I almost forgot the 111 Club which includes peaks in New York too.

We had our acceptance notice in hand but not our certificates; we would have to wait for the annual presentation ceremony.

Rick drove up to meet me on Saturday April 13, 2013 and we drove to Stratham, NH for the festivities. We checked-in at reception and were amazed at how many people were there. We later learned that over four hundred and fifty people qualified in 2012 for the award; most of them were in attendance and we were more than pleased to renew our acquaintance with a few people that we had met on the trail.

	Record of My Hiking the Four Thousand Footers in New Hampshire			
	Dr. Leonard J. Nyberg, Jr.			
Number	Mountain	Elevation	Date	Companion/Remarks
1	Adams	5,774	8/7/1965	Three times - REB/MJN/AC
2	Bond	4,698	7/6/2012	Rick
3	Bondcliff	4,265	7/6/2012	Rick
4	Cabot	4,170	5/18/2012	Rick
5	Cannon	4,100	9/11/1965	MJN
6	Carrigan	4,700	8/14/1965	MJN
7	Carter Dome	4,832	7/20/2012	Rick
8	East Osceola	4,156	8/1/1965	MJN/With Rick 8/3/2011
9	Eisenhower	4,780	9/1/2011	Rick
10	Field	4,340	7/30/2011	Rick
11	Flume	4,328	9/27/1965	MJN
12	Galehead	4,024	11/18/2011	Rick/Snow and Ice
13	Garfield	4,500	7/14/2011	Solo
14	Hale	4,054	7/27/2011	Solo/With Rick on 10/31/11 - Snow
15	Hancock	4,420	8/12/2011	Rick
16	Isolation	4,004	8/7/2012	Rick
17	Jackson	4,052	9/1/2011	Rick
18	Jefferson	5,712	8/7/1965	Three times - REB/MJN/AC
19	Lafayette	5,260	9/27/1965	MJN
20	Liberty	4,459	7/27/1965	MJN
21	Lincoln	5,089	9/29/1965	MJN
22	Madison	5,367	8/7/1965	Three times - REB/MJN/AC
23	Middle Carter	4,610	7/20/2012	Rick
24	Middle Tripyramid	4,140	5/25/2012	Rick
25	Monroe	5,384	8/7/1965	Three times - REB/MJN/AC
26	Moosilauke	4,802	7/5/2011	Bob (Twice)
27	Moriah	4,049	5/12/2012	Rick
28	North Kinsman	4,293	9/12/1965	MJN
29	North Tripyramid	4,180	12/2/2011	Rick (twice)
30	North Twin	4,761	7/19/2011	Solo
31	Osceola	4,340	8/3/2011	Rick
32	Owl's Head	4,025	8/14/2012	Rick
33	Passaconaway	4,043	9/16/2011	Rick
34	Pierce	4,310	9/1/2011	Rick
35	South Carter	4,430	7/20/2012	Rick
36	South Hancock	4,319	8/12/2011	Rick
37	South Kinsman	4,358	9/12/1965	MJN
38	South Twin	4,902	7/19/2011	Solo
39	Tecumseh	4,003	7/25/2011	Solo
40	Tom	4,051	7/30/2011	Solo - met Rick for 1st time on summit
41	Washington	6,288	9/3/1962	Three times - REB/MJN/AC
42	Waumbek	4,006	10/10/2011	Solo
43	West Bond	4,540	7/5/2012	Rick
44	Whiteface	4,020	6/1/2012	Rick
45	Wildcat	4,422	7/19/2012	Rick
46	Wildcat D	4,050	7/19/2012	Rick
47	Willey	4,285	7/30/2011	Rick
48	Zealand	4,260	7/5/2012	Rick

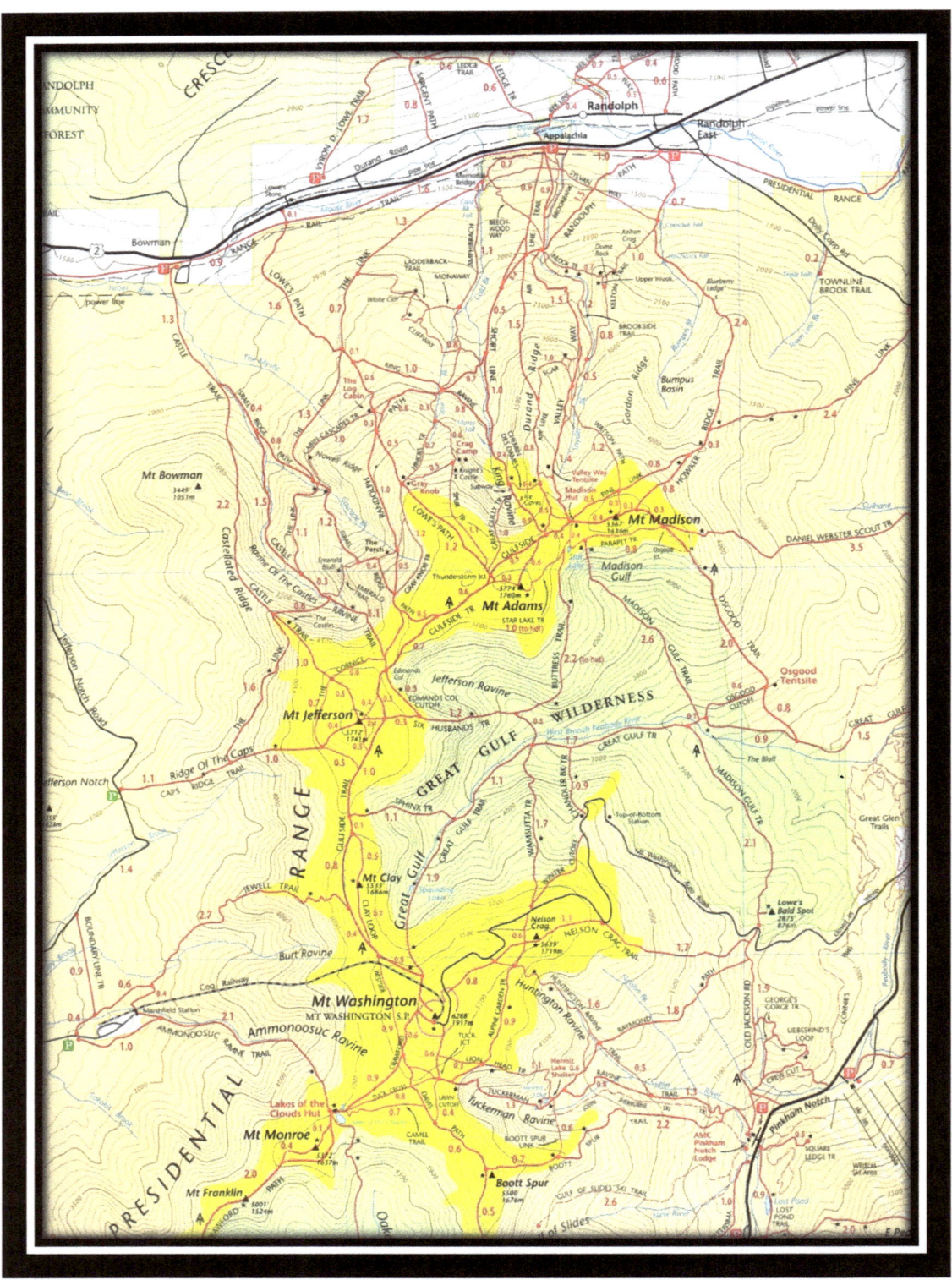

Portion of the Trail Map of the White Mountains, 4th Edition

Published by Map Adventures, LLC

The auditorium was pretty well packed with very few empty seats and, after an introduction of the committee members and a few remarks, the presentation began.

The presentations were made in "random" order and Rick was called before me.

It was great! Every time an award was presented it was met with applause and cheers and, no matter how many were given out, the enthusiasm never waned.

Of course some individuals and groups had their own cheering sections which added to the enjoyment.

Here is Rick's Certificate:

When my name was called it was also announced that I was the oldest member to receive a certificate this year – I was pleasantly amazed that I received a standing ovation in addition to the applause and cheers. All I could say was WOW!

My Certificate:

In the reception area there were a number of vendors selling maps, shirts, books and other stuff of interest to hikers – one of the vendors was our friend Nancy Sporborg who, with her friend Pat Piper, had written a great book entitled: *It's Not About The Hike – Two Ordinary Women on an Extraordinary Journey*. These two women have done it all; the NH 48, New England's Four Thousand Footers, New England's 100 Highest, and the peaks in New York. The photo above is of Rick with Nancy – I'm with Nancy in the photo below.

So, what's next for Rick and I? We have three peaks in Vermont and twelve in Maine to qualify for admission to the New England Four Thousand Footer Club – stay tuned!

AMC Four Thousand Footer Committee

An Enthusiastic Audience

Part II - And Beyond

The New Hampshire Four Thousand Footers, although fond memories, are now history and it's time to move on. I turned seventy-six on the 7th of September 2012 and celebrated the day with a solo hike up Blueberry Mountain; a week later I soloed Mt. Moosilauke for the third or fourth time.

I mentioned in an earlier section that I am an amateur radio enthusiast. In that capacity I was recently named as manager of a group of "Hams", as they are frequently called, known as the Green Mountain Net – it is the oldest continuing ham radio net currently on the air.

Each year we get together for a picnic; the last two years have been at our home in Lisbon, New Hampshire. There is a sub-division of the group known as the "good-old-boys" (GOBs) who meet contemporaneously with our picnics. The GOBs are a "select" group and are known for off-the-cuff presentations that are most often riddled with humor.

This past year was no exception and I was the recipient of the little known, but highly prestigious, mountaineering GOLDEN BOOT AWARD. I don't know this for a fact, but I believe that I am the only one in the world to have earned this spot in mountaineering history.

Here are some photographs of the award ceremony:

Here is the salute to the official GOB Flag. Note that I am wearing the robes of the Most Holy Inductor.

Also note that the "official" flag is a pair of polka dot shorts, and the flagstaff is topped with a toilet bowl float.

You are probably wondering where in the world the polka dot shorts came from – well, it's kind of a long story and probably too long a story to tell here; however, I can assure the reader that there was no violence, no bloodshed and no animals were abused or injured during the acquisition thereof.

Actually, they were standard get-together garb for fellow Green Mountain Net member Norm Diaz (shown at left) for many years – eventually, Norm decided to donate them to the cause and they now proudly fly on the flagstaff as the official banner of the GOBs.

In this photograph I am accepting the Golden Boot presented by the Exalted GOB Scribe.

It was a great honor for me to be awarded this prestigious symbol of mountaineering excellence; of course I was dutifully humbled by the presentation.

Although I was prepared for the first award, totally unbeknownst to me I was also to be honored with a second award that was to be presented after the close of the GOLDEN BOOT ceremony. This award was presented by the Exalted TGG/Grand GOB himself and, although I was overcome with emotion, I didn't faint or anything like that.

This award was contained in the UNHOLY GRAIL and naturally never touched by human hands prior to the actual presentation. The Grand GOB appropriately covered his hands with special gloves prior to handling the contents of the GRAIL.

In this photograph the Grand GOB is presenting the UNHOLY GRAIL to the recipient and the honored guests.

In this photograph I have been given the honor of unlocking the UNHOLY GRAIL.

This photo shows the presentation of the contents of the UNHOLY GRAIL to me and witnessed by the vast throng of honored and totally spellbound guests. The award was an official AMC Four Thousand Footer glass with all the mountains listed thereon.

A toast was appropriate – I am raising the award glass in humble appreciation of the duo of prestigious honors bestowed upon me that day.

It should be noted that the liquid in the glass is an 18 year old Single-Malt Scotch Whiskey - a fitting salute to the day's festivities.

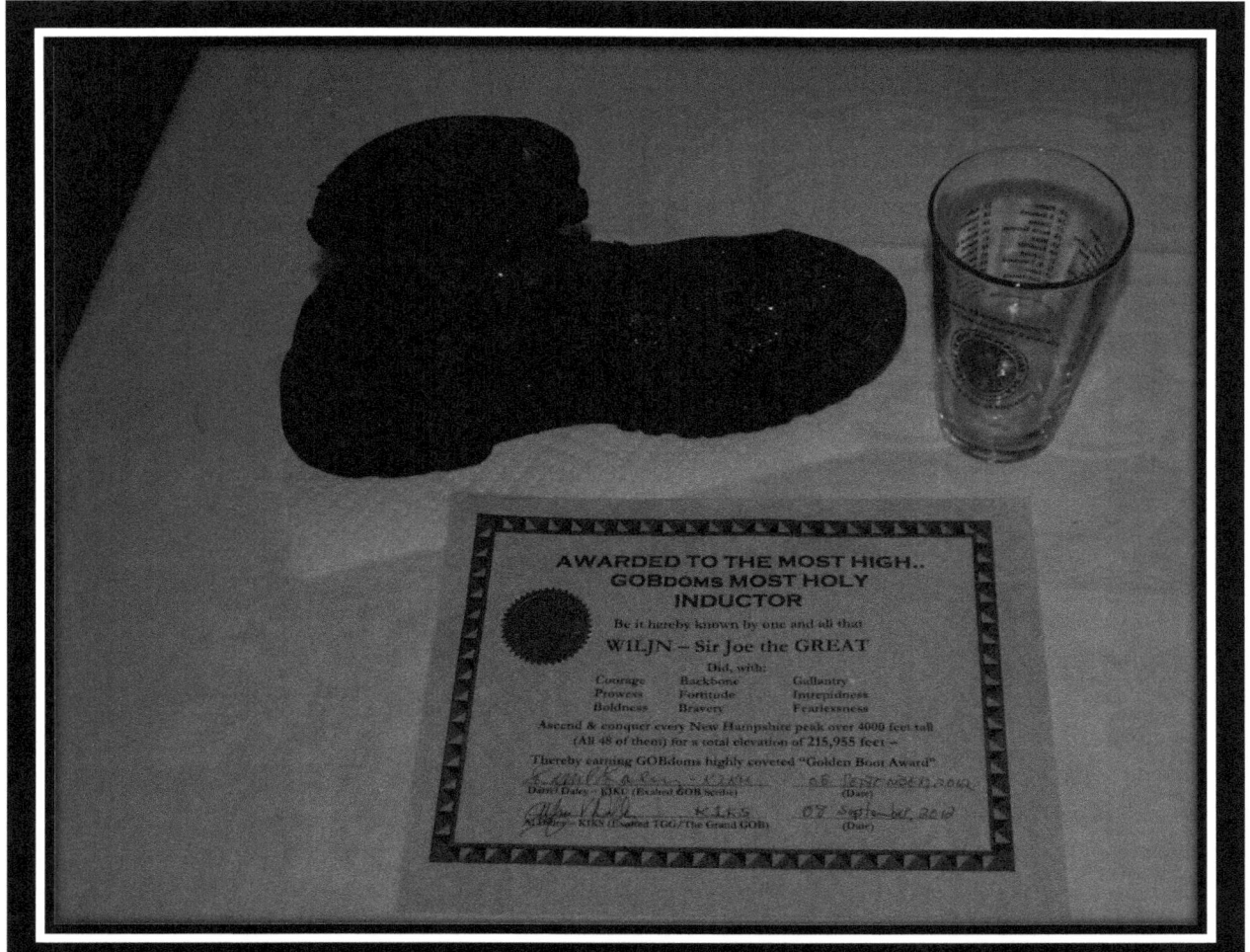

THE AWARDS

Now that the awards are safely framed and displayed, it is time to consider other adventures. We had completed hiking all forty-eight four thousand footers in NH – so, what's next. Well, Rick and I decided that we would attempt a couple of peaks on snowshoes – oh sure, we hiked a few last year in winter but were able to "bare boot" them all even with the snow.

But winter has not arrived yet, so what to do to fill in the gap? I know – Technical Rock Climbing! I haven't done this in several years so I retained the company of an expert, Charlie Townsend of Eastern Mountain Sports in North Conway.

After several email messages we decided on a date and time and my wife Dawn and I checked into the North Conway Grand Hotel the night before the adventure.

At 0830 hrs. the following day, we met Charlie and after I got outfitted with helmet, harness and rock climbing shoes, we headed out. Originally we had planned to climb Cathedral Ledge but

Charlie suggested that, because of the temperature and the fact that Cathedral Ledge would be in the shade most of the day, we would be better advised to climb the neighboring Whitehorse Ledge.

In this photograph I'm anchored to the rock and belaying Charlie on the second pitch and playing out the safety rope. The rope is sixty meters in length and Charlie sets two more anchors at equal distances on his way up the second pitch – this is a safety factor to minimize the distance of a fall or slip should one occur. Once he is anchored he will belay me and, on my way up to meet him, I will dislodge the anchors and take them with me to meet him. We'll then start the process all over again on the next pitch.

In this photograph I am leaving the second pitch and heading for number three; Charlie is belaying me from the ledges above and also taking some great photos.

Cathedral Ledge is over my right shoulder. Whitehorse Ledge is about three hundred feet higher than Cathedral Ledge – both are about the same difficulty.

Here I am belaying Charlie and getting ready to rappel down to the second pitch level. We had two ropes and for the rappel down Charlie tied the two together and used a "fireman's belay" as a safety measure for my trip back down. Once we were back to the lower level we retrieved both ropes for the last rappel back to where we started.

Here I am at the halfway point on the rappel down.

I'm back at the starting point - the conclusion of a Great Day!

Dawn told me that I looked like a telephone lineman.

On November 6th, Rick and I decided to do a little hiking and met early in the morning at the Willey House Site parking area on Route 302 in Crawford Notch. Rick left his truck there and we proceeded to Zealand Notch, leaving my car in the parking area at the Zealand Trail trailhead.

The temperature was in the low teens and there was about four inches of new snow on the ground when we put on our packs and headed south on the Zealand Trail. Even with the snow we made very good time and reached Zealand Pond in an hour and thirty minutes.

From here we followed the Ethan Pond Trail and soon came to the rock slide on the western slope of Whitewall Mountain (3,405') – from here we had a clear view of Zeacliff to the west and the Zealand Hut to our north. In another 0.8 mile we reached the Thoreau Falls Trail and hiked the short distance to the top of the falls (left).

In this view of the falls, the white area in the foreground is an icecap.

Here is a photograph of Rick in the clearing by the upper falls.

The photograph below is a view from the falls looking west toward Mt. Guyot and the Bonds. The visibility was somewhat restricted by falling and blowing snow.

After a short break we continued on the Ethan Pond Trail and soon crossed a newly constructed footbridge over the brook that flows from Ethan Pond, about two miles further east. Although there was about four inches of new snow on the ground, the trail from here to the pond was very wet and not easy going.

We eventually reached the pond, crossed the east end and took a short spur to the Ethan Pond Shelter, a three sided Adirondak Style shelter located on a high point northeast of the pond.

Here's Rick at the shelter.

And here's me.

This was our last hike during the 2012 season.

2013

We had no hiking adventures during the first two months of the new year and, although we had done some walking, Rick in Milford and me here in New Hampshire, walking ain't hiking! I must admit that the weather during the winter months was not really conducive to hiking so we kept a very low profile during this period.

In early March I found myself suffering from "cabin fever" and the weather forecast for Saturday March 8th looked promising, so I packed the Jeep with my hiking gear and headed for Crawford Notch and a "cobweb clearing" hike up Mt. Willard (2,865'). Now this hike is not a Herculean task by any means and this was my third trip to the summit; it was, at least in my estimation, a good way to shake the cobwebs out and get back into the swing of things.

The day was totally awesome! I couldn't have asked God for a better one – the sky was cloudless and a beautiful blue and the contrast between the sky, the white of the snow on the upper peaks and the woods of the mountainsides was breathtaking.

I brought micro-spikes with me but, since it was Saturday and a popular spot for weekend hikers, I was able to "bare-boot" the entire trail, both up and return.

The trail begins at the Crawford Station as the A-Z Trail but soon the Mt. Willard Trail bears off to the left; the distance to the summit is 1.6 miles.

Even in the poor shape that I was in, I made the trip up in one hour and fifteen minutes (1.3 MPH) but rocketed back down in twenty-five minutes (4 MPH).

After hiking a half-mile, there is a short spur to the right that leads to Centennial Falls – during the warmer months this is a very scenic waterfall and pool; however, today no falls, pool or any water whatsoever could be seen.

From here the trail follows the old carriage road to the summit.

This is a photograph of Mt. Willard looking north from Crawford Notch and Route 302. The cliffs are a popular spot for technical rock climbers; two reached the summit while I was there.

The views from the summit were spectacular to say the least; visibility was unlimited and there was not a blemish in the sky. In this photo the Mount Washington summit can be seen at right center.

Here is a view to the south; Webster Cliffs can be seen to the left, the east slope of Mt. Willey on the right, Route 302 center, the RR tracks through Crawford's on the right, and in the distance in the center of the photo is Mt. Chocorua in Tamworth, NH, about 30 miles south.

Of course I would be remiss if I didn't include a photo of myself at the summit.

Mt Webster (3,910') is at the upper right of the photo.

I spent over two hours at the summit and really could have stayed longer; I was just a spectacular day and, sadly, I am at a loss of words to adequately describe it.

The rest of this month I'll spend getting back into hiking shape, right now the snow is disappearing quite rapidly and, although there is a good possibility of snow during the rest of March, we're hoping that by the first part of April the weather will allow us to resume our hiking adventures.

Right now our plan is to complete the New England's Four Thousand Footers; we have completed all of New Hampshire but still need three in Vermont and twelve in Maine so it looks like a busy hiking season coming up. After we complete all of the four thousand footers, we're hoping to attack the One Hundred New England Highest.

Well, April lingered on with weather not conducive to hiking; however, there were a couple of other events that are well worth mentioning.

On April 8th my friend Monica joined me for a hike to the ancient Mt. Cilley Settlement in what is now Woodstock. I have been exploring this area for the past six years and have located and identified several cellar holes that have been in existence for over two hundred years*. The hike wasn't a particularly long one but we encountered knee deep snow during most of it.

Here is Monica on the ancient road just below the cellar hole that once belonged to Matthew P. Hunt, one of the largest landowners of the settlement.

Here I am at the same place. We plan to go back during the summer to find the last of the cellar holes. According to a survey made in the mid 1860's, there were ten cellar holes at that time; to date I have located and identified eight of them, including what was once the school.

Here's Monica sitting on the corner of the M. P. Hunt foundation.

The Ancient Road below Hunt's

May was just a bit more promising but still was not the best weather for our plans. The mountains in Vermont still had considerable snow and the Green Mountain Club discouraged hiking the upper peaks until after the dreaded "mud season" had passed. So, considering the fact that both of us were suffering from "cabin fever", we decided to begin adding peaks that qualify for New England's One Hundred Highest and mix them in with the New England Four Thousand Footers.

Consequently, on May 13th we headed out early to attack North Weeks Mountain (3,901'). North Weeks is located in the Pliny Range which includes Mounts Starr King, Waumbek, and the three peaks of Weeks. We arrived at the trailhead at 0630 hrs. and started the 3.7 mile trek to the summit. The air temperature was thirty-nine degrees and, although it snowed lightly the entire day, thankfully there was no accumulation.

We planned to follow the York Pond Trail for 2.4 miles before branching off to the south on the Killkenny Ridge Trail that would take us to the summit. The beginning of the trail followed an old lumber road through Willard Notch and follows a brook with several crossings along the way. At 2.4 miles the junction of the York Pond and Kilkenney Ridge Trails is reached; the former continues to a dead end and the latter to the south – it should be noted that the trail dead ends because one of the landowners decided not to allow foot traffic over his portion of the trail.

I was able to manage a smile -   **BUT……Rick needed something to hold him up.**

The trail continues in a general southerly direction for 1.3 miles and rises rather steeply before finally reaching the summit of North Weeks. Several patches of snow were encountered on this section of the trail but no special equipment was necessary.

Although there were a few openings along the trail where Mt. Cabot and The Horn could be seen through the trees, most of the trail and the summit were in the woods with no views.

Rick and me at the Summit (Tired? Who Me? Someone had to hold that tree up!)

Although the hike up went rather slowly because I was painfully out of shape, the trip down went rather well and we made pretty good time.

The photo at right is The Horn (3.905'), a peak that is on the N.E. 100 Highest list – more on that later.

I have mentioned brook crossings before:

Back, in an earlier section of this book when I was discussing the hike up to Middle Tripyramid (Page 29), you may recall that Rick had to construct a "bridge" so I could cross the river – well he did it again. This "bridge" was a little less in span than the other but it still kept the old man's feet dry and was as much appreciated as the last time it was necessary.

Rick was a little more agile and rock-hopped across.

It was a long day but it was great to get back in the woods and get another peak "for the count".

On May 16th we made an attempt to attack The Horn (3,905'), another on the N.E. 100 Highest list. We decided to take the Unknown Pond Trail from Stark and then the Kilkenney Ridge Trail from the pond to the spur that would take us to the Horn. We took this same trail last year when we hiked Mt. Cabot; during that hike we could have easily taken the short spur to the Horn but decided not to – oh well, 20/20 hindsight.

Well, yours truly was painfully out of shape and slow – just like Mt. Moriah last year when my legs felt like lead and I had difficulty getting my "second wind". We finally arrived at Unknown Pond and, when it appeared that a storm was brewing to the west of us, we decided to head back and try the Horn at a later date.

I'm not saying that the rest was well deserved, but I will say that it was well received. It's amazing how comfortable rocks can be at a time like this.

Even though it was mid-May, there was still snow on the shore of the pond – we encountered some snow on the trail but not enough to hinder our progress in any way.

Unknown Pond is near the 2,800' contour and is a beautiful pond with a small campground nearby. There are several views of the Horn from the east shore.

Here is a photo of the Horn looking southwest.

Here's Rick checking out the Horn with his binoculars.

Here I am resting again – what else is new?

We finally left the pond and headed back to the parking area where we had left our vehicles. Although the trail was rocky and wet and roots were plentiful, we had an enjoyable day even though we failed in our attempt to add another peak to our list.

ON TO VERMONT!

As I mentioned earlier, there is a total of five peaks to climb in Vermont in order to complete the Vermont Four Thousand Footers – the list of the peaks follows:

Mt. Abraham, 4,006' - Camel's Hump, 4,083' – Mt. Ellen, 4,083' – Killington Peak, 4,235' and Mt. Mansfield (The Chin), 4,393'

Both Rick and I have climbed Camel's Hump and Mt. Mansfield, so only three remain for us.

But first we have to wait for the snow to melt and after that the dreaded "mud season" arrives. If you live in northern New England, mud season is something that we never look forward to – after the snow melts and only a couple of inches of ground have thawed, melting snow and rain make the dirt roads almost impassable; an old Vermonter once described it as "….driving through peanut butter……". Well, the same thing happens with many of the hiking trails, particularly in the higher elevations.

GMC trails closed for mud

It's been mud season on The Valley floor for several weeks now, so it's easy to forget that snow takes longer to melt in the mountains.

On Monday, April 15, the Green Mountain Club (GMC) announced the start of mud season on Vermont's higher elevation hiking trails. During this time, the club discourages hikers from taking these routes in order to minimize damage due to erosion and the trampling of vegetation.

"Every step not taken on a wet hiking trail today helps assure a stable tread way tomorrow and reduce future costly tread repairs," GMC executive director Will Wiquist said, as it's important that trails have the time to drain and dry before they experience heavy use this season.

Hiking trails on land managed by the Vermont Department of Forests, Parks and Recreation and the Green Mountain Club are closed until Memorial Day. Hikers are also strongly discouraged from using hiking trails in the Green Mountain National Forest. Generally, along the route of the Long Trail, the national forest exists south from Mt. Ellen in Warren and the state parks and forests exist north of Appalachian Gap in Buel's Gore.

In the meantime, however, hikers are encouraged to explore trails at lower elevations. General guidelines for hiking during mud season: Walk through the mud, not around it. If it's too deep to walk through, then turn around!

This notice appeared in the local newspaper; other notices can be found on the Green Mountain Club website and other news publications.

In some cases the trails are actually closed.

I waited until mud season was over; this year the rains extended the season and it was mid-June before a real break came.

On Saturday June 15th, I was suffering from cabin fever and desired to hit the trail; unfortunately, Rick was in the middle of a move and could not join me. So, I packed my gear and left the house at 0600 hrs. and headed for Jerusalem, VT.

The trip took me through the Appalachian Gap and Buel's Gore, an interesting settlement located on Route 17. Buel's Gore was originally chartered on November 4, 1780 and was named after Major Elias Buel. The town contains a total of five square miles with a total population of thirty, according to the 2010 census, more than double than the population in 2000 of twelve. When I lived in Vermont back in the late 1960's and early 1970's, the population was said to be two.

Route 17 winds its way through the gap and eventually reaches the town of Jerusalem where the trailhead is located at an elevation of 1,628' – the trail ascends through a stand of hardwoods, predominantly maple, for about 2.2 miles before a steep ascent to the junction of the Long Trail. This trail follows the main ridge of the Green Mountains for a distance of about two hundred and seventy miles, stretching from the Canadian Border to the Massachusetts State line.

A sign at the trailhead announces that the trail passes through privately owned land and care should be taken to ensure future use.

As I mentioned earlier, the predominant species of trees is the maple and as the trail ascends it is obvious that hundreds, if not thousands, of these trees are tapped for maple sugaring purposes. Miles of plastic tubing, 2.5" PVC piping, pumps and various other evidence of sugaring can be seen along the trail.

The lower portion of the trail is actually the access road for the maintenance of the sugaring lines, pumps and other equipment.

At about two miles the trail narrows, steepens and the maple trees become mixed with non-deciduous types and the sugaring operation ceases.

At 2.4 miles the trail reaches the junction with the Long Trail; the elevation here is 3,430' and there are few viewpoints between here and the summit of Mt. Ellen (4,083'). The view at left was taken about a tenth of a mile from the junction – it is facing south. The distance from the trail junction to the summit is 1.8 miles.

The summit is also the top of a popular ski area; the ski lift terminates near the summit which is a popular spot for hikers to stop for a lunch break or just a rest. The view from here is spectacular; Lake Champlain can be seen to the northwest, the Adirondacks of New York can be seen to the west, Canada can be seen to the north and New Hampshire can be seen to the southeast.

This photograph of me at the top of the ski lift was taken by a young woman who I met at the summit. She and her young daughter were hiking the Long Trail from Lincoln Gap to Appalachian Gap, a distance of 11.6 miles and covering seven peaks, two of which are in excess of four thousand feet.

This panorama photograph is looking northwest and west – Lake Champlain can be seen just below the horizon and the peaks to the left of the photo are in the Adirondack Mountains in Upstate New York.

This view is facing east from the summit and the peak to the right of the tree in the foreground is Camel's Hump.

The woman who took my photograph at the summit was hiking with her young daughter – I guessed her age at about six or seven; she carried her pack from Appalachian Gap to Mt. Abraham (4,006'), a distance of 2.6 miles, before deciding it was a little too much - wherein her mom attached her pack to that of her own. They were planning to spend the night at Stark's Nest, a distance of two miles. I passed them on the trail and later when I was taking a break at the junction of the Long Trail and Jerusalem Trail we met again. I requested a photo but didn't dare ask if she could add my pack to her load.

After some fresh pineapple I headed back down the trail to the parking area; some of the trail was dry but much of it was wet and muddy. The conditions pictured in the photograph below continued for a little over a mile.

It was a long, but very enjoyable day.

Rain, rain and more rain has been the rule rather than the exception for the past few weeks and it has surely dampened (pun intended) our efforts but not our spirits to conquer the remaining peaks to complete all of the New England four thousand footers.

Well, I kept a very close eye on the weather and the report from Burlington suggested that Friday, July 12th would be an ideal day to head for the Green Mountains for a hike up Mt. Abraham (4,006').

I should mention that the National Weather Service in Burlington, VT has a great site for the high peaks in the Green Mountains. All you need to do is to bring up the site and click on the mountain that you are interested in or the one closest to it; in this case it was neighboring Mt. Ellen.

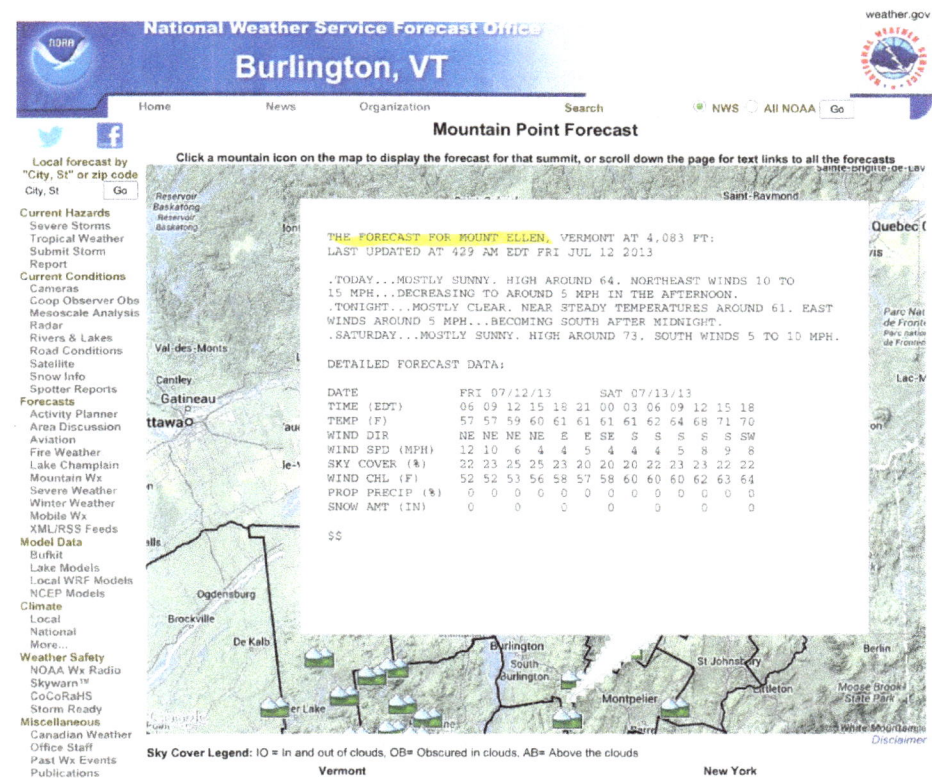

I called Rick on Wednesday evening and he agreed to meet me in Lisbon at 0630 hrs.- from there we would drive together for the day's adventure. We left the house at about 0700 hrs. and headed for the trailhead at Lincoln Gap (2,424'), near the town of Warren, VT. The two hour drive gave us plenty of time to discuss our next adventure before heading to Maine for the last dozen peaks.

From the trailhead the Long Trail ascends in a northerly direction and soon begins a steady ascent. At 1.2 miles the trail passes between the Carpenters, two large boulders named after a pair of trail workers.

Shortly after the Carpenters, a very interesting thing happened. We had met several other hikers along the way and stopped to chat with almost all of them; however, we soon met a trio of women who during our chat mentioned that they were members of the AMC Four Thousand Footer Club. Well, Rick asked if they were present at the award ceremony last April – the answer was in the affirmative. That prompted Rick to ask if they remembered that I received a standing ovation when it was announced that I was the oldest hiker to receive the 2012 award – "YES," they replied – "we were sitting right behind you in the auditorium." That led to a further remark that they were in fact talking about that very thing before we met on the trail. Coincidence? Maybe, but it is a reminder that it really IS a small world after all.

It wouldn't be fair not to include Rick in the photo; after all he is also a fellow member of the AMC Four Thousand Footer Club.

The trail continues for another half-mile before reaching its junction with the Battell Trail, a two mile trail named after Joseph Battell (1839-1915). Joseph Battell was a publisher and philanthropist from Middlebury, Vermont and is credited with preserving Vermont forest land including Camel's Hump State Park. He authored a book entitled *Ellen, or the Whisperings of an Old Pine*, a dialogue between a sixteen year-old girl and a wise old white pine tree. Among the

illustrations included therein are the subject, Ellen Gardiner, and her mountain, Mt. Ellen (4,083'), one of the five peaks along the Long Trail that are in excess of four thousand feet.

One tenth of a mile past the intersection is the Battell Shelter, an Adirondack style shelter that sleeps eight.

In just a few minutes we arrived at the Battell Shelter and found six or eight young girls in residence with their two adult counselors. We rested for a while before heading further up the trail.

Here's Rick at the shelter.

From here we had a hike of 0.9 miles before we reached the summit, the last quarter mile or so being quite rocky and steep; with the recent rains the trail was quite wet in places and caution had to be a priority on the steep rocks and bare ledge. It was 1300 hrs. when we reached the summit which afforded a three hundred sixty degree view - Canada north, New York west and New Hampshire east.

The photo above is a view of the trail just below the bare ledge that leads to the summit; the angle of the trees will give the reader an idea of the steepness of the trail.

In this photograph Rick and I are sitting on the rocks on the summit; behind us can be seen some of the New Hampshire peaks.

The day was glorious and the visibility was more than fifty miles. There was some haze but not enough to detract from the view.

This is a photograph of two old dogs at the summit discussing their adventures in the mountains – my friend was seventy-seven years old in dog years and, of course, in just a few weeks I'll be seventy-seven years old in human years.

We had a lot to talk about but soon it became time to make our return trip to the parking area and I had to bid my old friend farewell and Godspeed.

Our discussion reminded me of the many years that my faithful German Shepherd was my companion on hikes such as this.

Looking Southeast from Just Below the Summit   **Looking South**

Our descent went much faster than our ascent and we arrived back at the parking area at 1630 hrs. Our next adventure will be Mt. Killington (4,235')

"Go where he will, the wise man is at home,
His hearth the earth, - his hall the azure dome;
Where his clear spirit leads him, there's his road,
By God's own light illumined and foreshowed."
Emerson

The 17th of July proved to be a glorious day for hiking, so Rick arrived at our home at 0630 hrs. and we set off for Mendon, VT for a hike up Killington Peak (4,235'), the last of the four thousand foot peaks in Vermont.

Rick's Ready

I'm Still Thinking About It

First Brewer Brook Crossing

We arrived at the Bucklin Trail trailhead at 0830 hrs. and began our trek. The first part of the trail is rather easy and follows the old carriage road; in a short distance it crosses Brewer's Brook and continues east along the old woods road. In just over a mile it once again crosses the brook and after another mile begins a steady climb out of the valley to the intersection of the Bucklin, Appalachian and Long Trails, about 3.4 miles from the start.

Both brook crossings were very easy - most times we either wade across or rock hop. Today there were two extremely well-built bridges, the first of which you could drive a cement truck over. Here is Rick resting on the stairs.

From the last crossing the trail increases in difficulty and finally reaches the Long Trail at 3.4 miles.

Two other trail signs mark the spot:

From the intersection the trail continues in a generally southeasterly direction for about 0.2 miles to the Cooper Lodge, a stone structure built in 1939 with a capacity of about ten to twelve people. In this photo Rick is shown with "Radar", the trail name of a "through" hiker with a goal of hiking the entire Appalachian Trail. All through hikers take on a "trail name".

Interior View

Well, I really wouldn't refer to the lodge as a resort, but I suppose it depends on the time of day and, of course, the weather conditions.

I spotted this sign on a tree near the lodge and immediately pictured a nice deep pool with picnic tables and umbrellas, perhaps even a lifeguard. If we were really lucky, maybe even a few bathing beauties lying around soaking up the sun.

However…………………..

It turned out to be a spring with a pool about four inches deep; of course the best part was that the water was clear and cold – very cold and very welcoming on a warm day in July.

From the lodge and its ancillary accouterments, the trail continued southwesterly and steeply for another 0.2 mile, the last 0.1 being the usual rock scramble. Hiking mountains would be absolutely no fun if there weren't big rocks and steep ledges that the hiker had to manipulate before reaching the elusive summit. This summit was no exception – was the view worth the effort? Of course! When we arrived at the summit we encountered several people dressed rather casually and who didn't really have the appearance of hikers – we soon learned that they arrived from the ski area below via gondolas – why hadn't we thought of that? They even brought nicely wrapped hamburgers for sustenance on their arduous journey; however, they lacked the sense of excitement experienced in hiking up the trail for four plus hours, swatting off flies and bugs and scrambling up rocks for the last quarter mile – they don't know what they missed, do they?

The other thing that they missed was chalking up peak number fifty-five (on foot).

We now have twelve more peaks to conquer before completing our current goal of all of the New England Four Thousand Foot peaks.

The other thing they missed, of course, was the last 0.1 mile rock scramble to the summit.

I suppose that they could have done it but they would have to put their nicely wrapped hamburgers in their pockets.

Views from the summit:

On the way back down we saw an interesting sight:

There was a young man who lived in a tree.

And so we bid farewell to the Green Mountains of Vermont

HELLO to the Mountains of Maine –

There is a total of fourteen peaks in Maine that are in excess of four thousand feet:

Mt. Abraham (4,050')
Bigelow Mountain, Avery Peak (4,090')
Bigelow Mountain, West Peak (4,145')
Crocker Mountain (4,228')
Crocker Mountain South Peak (4,050')
Katahdin Baxter Peak (5,268')
Katahdin Hamlin Peak (4,756')
North Brother (4,151')
Old Speck Mountain (4,170')
Redington Mountain (4,010')
Saddleback Mountain (4,120')
Saddleback Mountain, The Horn (4,041')
Spaulding Mountain (4,010')
Sugarloaf Mountain (4,250')

Since Rick and I have both climbed Katahdin Baxter and Hamlin Peaks, we have twelve peaks remaining. Our plan is to hike them in order of distance from home, so the first on the list is North Brother. From there we hope to hike the Bigelows; after that it would appear that the Crockers and Redington will be next in line, but that's long-range planning for now.

So, the countdown begins:

12, 11, 10, 9, 8, 7, 6, 5, 4, 3, 2, DONE!

The weather report for North Brother for Wednesday July 31st looked favorable for a hike, so I called and reserved a tent spot at the Nesowadnehunk Stream wilderness camp site in Baxter State Park in northern Maine.

Rick arrived in Lisbon at around 0930 hrs. and, after packing the Jeep, we were ready to depart at 1100 hrs. After a drive of six and one-half hours we arrived at the Baxter State Park gate house to check in for our stay. Our campsite was another hour drive along a narrow dirt road with a maximum speed limit of 20 MPH.

Baxter State Park was a gift to the people of Maine from Gov. Percival P. Baxter, who used his personal wealth over a 32-year period to purchase and donate the original 201,018 acres of the park. Since Gov. Baxter's death in 1969 the park has been increased to a total of 209,501 acres, including the 2006 addition of a parcel of 4,678 acres and spectacular Katahdin Lake. There are no stores or gas stations inside the park, access and uses are strictly regulated in accordance with Gov. Baxter's expressed desire to keep the Park "forever wild".

Inside the Park boundary electricity, running water, and paved roads are nonexistent. In keeping with the "Forever Wild" philosophy expressed by the Park donor Percival Baxter, the Park prohibits the use of audio or visual devices in any way that impairs the enjoyment of the Park by others or that may disturb or harass wildlife.

We eventually arrived at our campsite and checked in with the Ranger; our assigned campsite was No. 22 and we soon found that it was occupied by two women, three tents and several children. When I inquired why her party was still there, she replied that she was a holdover and had reserved another site across the field – we agreed to trade and take Site 20, checking with the Ranger to see if that was OK with her. In the meantime, Rick had discovered a small lean-to on the Doubletop Mountain Trail, just a few meters south of campsite #20 – we asked if that was available and were answered in the affirmative. So, Rick occupied the lean-to and I elected to sleep in the rear of our Jeep.

It seemed that I wasn't the only person that had elected to sleep in his vehicle, the fellow parked next to us slept in his as well – at least I had room in the back of mine, but his was quite a bit smaller and it seemed that his feet would extend into the trunk section of the vehicle.

In any event, the night went by pleasantly and at about midnight the heavens were alive with stars – it was an absolutely beautiful sight.

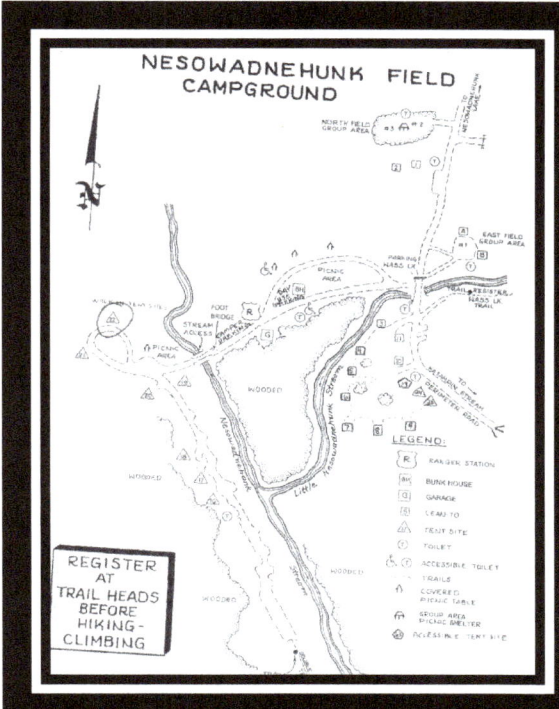

This is a map of the campground; the site that was assigned to us is circled at left center and the lean-to that Rick occupied was on the trail southeast of that location – I occupied the back of our Jeep in the parking area.

This photograph was taken from the bridge connecting the parking area to the campsites and is looking south. The peaks in the background are West Peak (2,502') and Mt. OJI (3,434').

Rick appeared at the car at 0522 hrs. and, after getting our hiking gear ready, we headed four miles south to the Marston Trail and the trailhead for North Brother Mountain.

All hikers are requested to sign in before hiking with the date and time of the start and then sign out after the hike was completed. The park rangers keep a careful eye out for campers and hikers to make certain that each person is accounted for and stays safe during their visit to the park.

Here is Rick signing us in at the register.

Here we are ready to conquer #56

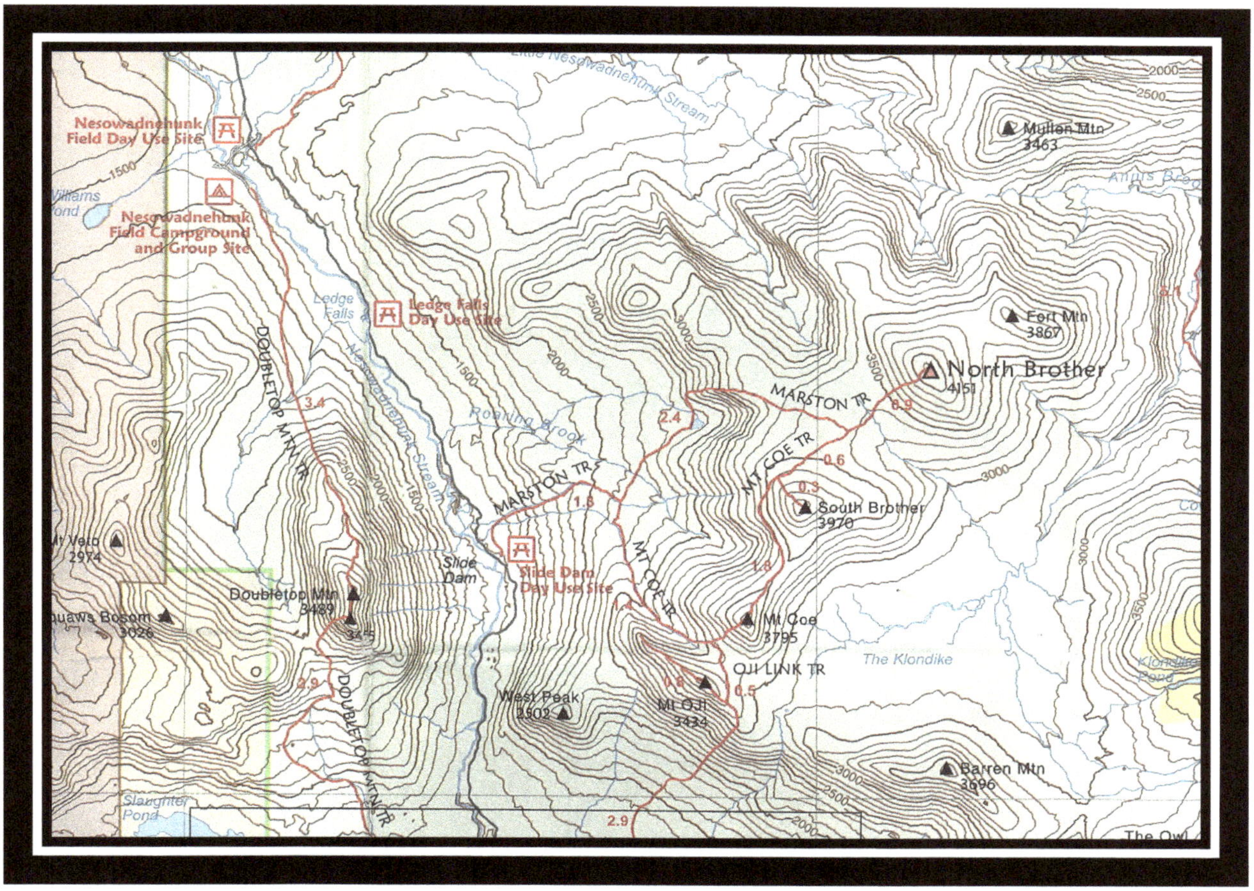

The Marston Trail is 5.2 miles in length with a change in elevation of approximately three thousand feet. The first 1.3 miles rises moderately to the junction of the Marston and Mt. Coe Trails at about 2,100 feet.

Here we are at the first Trail Junction.

From this point the trail turns in a general northeasterly direction and is relatively level for the next 1.2 miles before reaching Teardrop Pond, a small pond at the foot of the next pitch. From there the trail rises five hundred feet in 0.3 mile, a grade of approximately 30%.

Teardrop Pond

The next trail junction is the Marston and Mt. Coe Trail intersection and is about 1.2 miles from the pond; from the 3,000 foot contour the trail is relatively level to the trail junction.

A word of explanation may be in order at this point – both trail junctions are the intersections of the Marston and Mt. Coe Trails; that's because the Mt. Coe Trail is really a loop that begins at the first intersection, loops around Mt. Coe (3,975') and South Brother (3,970'), and rejoins the Marston Trail 0.8 miles from the summit of North Brother.

The trail proceeds in a general northeasterly direction and is relatively level for about 0.4 miles before climbing steeply to the summit of North Brother – the elevation change is 651 feet in 0.4 miles, or another grade of about 30%. The first half through a rough and narrow trail and, beyond the tree line, the last 0.2 miles is over large boulders.

The photograph above illustrates the rocky trail to the summit – the summit sign can be seen in the center of the photo just slightly to the left of the tallest rock by the edge of the clouds.

Here's Rick at the summit; the wind was blowing at about thirty knots.

After six hours on the trail, I found some soft rocks and elected to take a short nap.

After a brief rest I decided to brave the wind and posed for a photograph by the summit sign.

Here is a view of Mt. Katahdin (5,267') looking southeast from the summit of North Brother.

After a brief visit at the summit we headed back down the trail to the parking area; it was a long day – twelve hours of hiking, but the trip was worth it. This was peak number fifty-six out of a total of sixty seven – eleven more to go to reach our goal.

11, 10, 9, 8, 7, 6, 5, 4, 3, 2, DONE!

After a layoff of a month we decided to get back to our hiking plan; the weather for September fourth looked ideal so we headed for the Grafton Notch State Park and Old Speck Mountain (4,170').

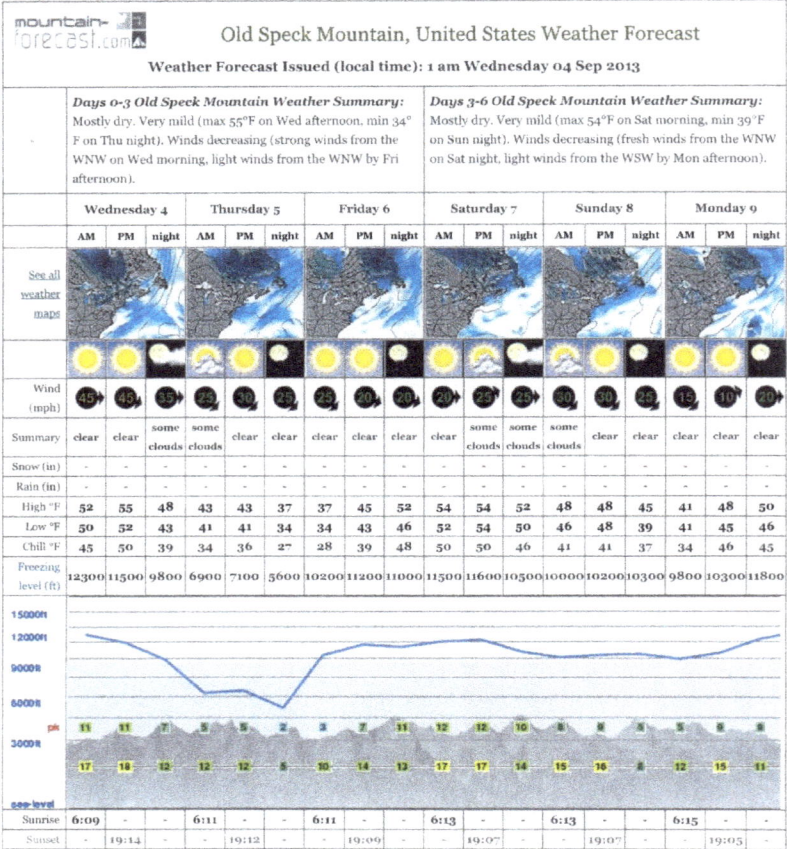

The forecast was for clear skies with summit temperatures in the fifties. The only negative was forty MPH winds; however, almost of the trail was in the woods so wind wouldn't be much of a factor until we reached the summit.

Well, Rick worked until 2300 hrs. the night before, went home and took a shower, and went to bed for a couple of hours before heading up to New Hampshire to meet me. I spoke with him on the phone at 0515 hrs., discovered that he was close by and soon he arrived at the house; in a half hour we were on the road and two hours later we were at the trailhead.

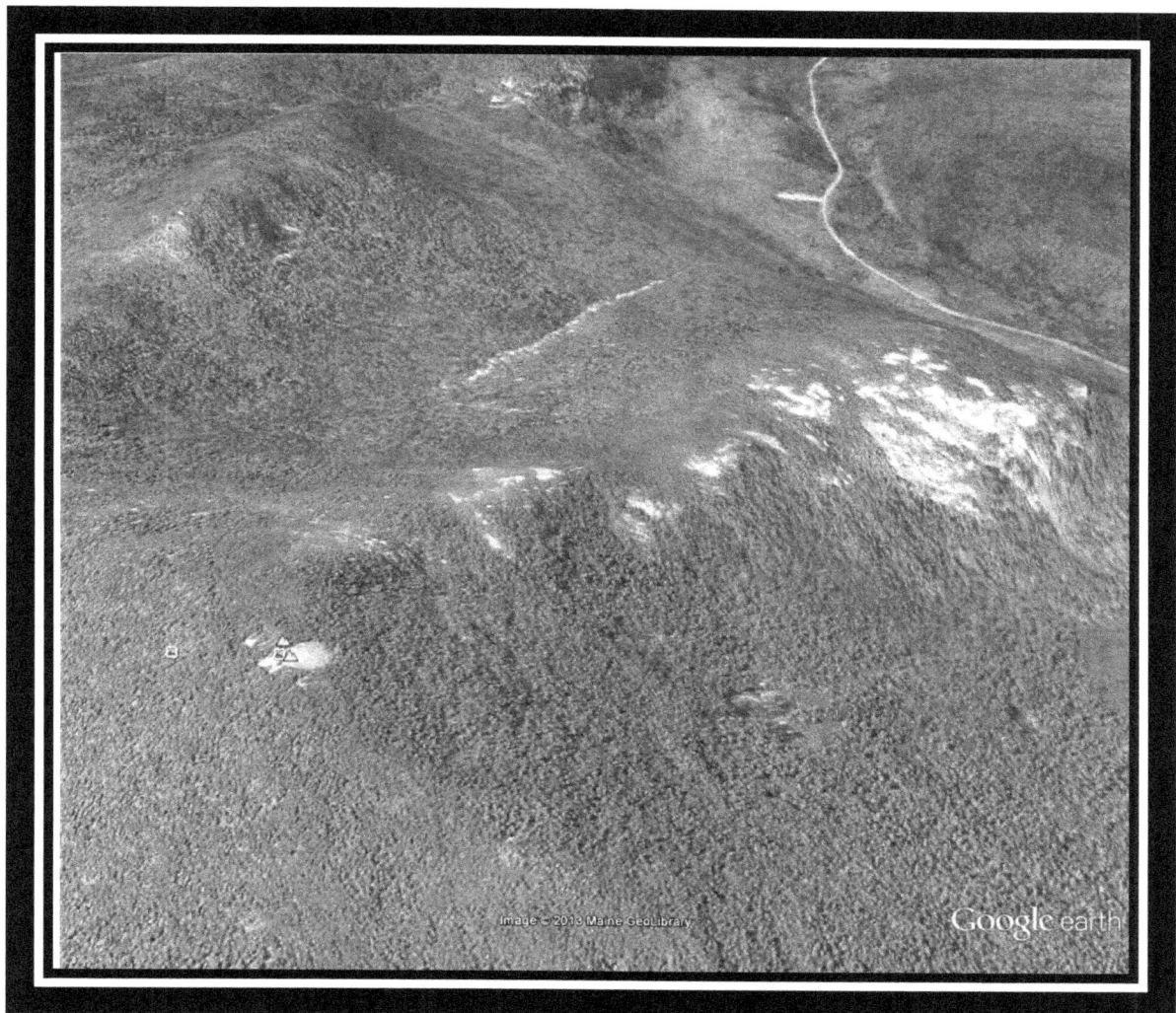

Satellite image of the summit of Old Speck (lower left arrows and clearing) – parking area and trailhead can be seen at upper right on the west side of Highway 26 and the Eyebrow ledges appear top center. The trail skirts the south side of the Eyebrow before following the ridge shown at the upper left.

The Dynamic Duo at the Trailhead

After a couple of photos we were on the Old Speck Trail, which is part of the Appalachian Trail System that extends from Georgia to Maine. The trail soon crosses a brook which it follows for about a mile before the second and last crossing. There were several waterfalls along the route, the most scenic one is pictured below.

From here the trail crosses a large ledge with open views before reaching the junction with the Eyebrow Trail, a 1.2 mile loop that crosses an 800 foot cliff; the use of handholds and ladders is necessary when hiking this trail – we elected to save this one for a future hike after we have completed all of the New England Four Thousand Foot Peaks.

On our way to the summit we met at least a dozen "through hikers", hikers who are on the last leg of completing the entire Appalachian Trail; many of them had begun their trek in Georgia last March.

From this point, the next trail junction was 2.4 miles away and part way Rick got his second wind and surged ahead on his own.

In a little over a mile I decided that it was time for a break and I found a comfortable rock ledge to sit on, check my altimeter and map and have a drink of water. It was just a few minutes later that I heard someone behind me and saw a young woman who was hiking solo; she stopped and sat with me for a while. She introduced herself as Paula and told me that she had hiked this mountain several times before – she is a computer wizard at the MIT Lincoln Laboratories in Cambridge, MA and was hiking alone because her hiking companion had to work and couldn't meet her until the following day.

Anyway, we agreed to hike to the summit together and discussed just about everything imaginable. I spoke about my hiking adventures with Rick and all we had accomplished to that point – after

about an hour or so, since we hadn't caught up with him, she began to suspect that Rick might have been a figment of my imagination and did not exist; well, when we reached the next trail junction, 0.3 miles from the summit, there was Rick waiting for me. Naturally he had already been to the summit but joined us for the last leg.

Rick and I at the Summit

Paula and I at the Summit

After some lunch and a few photos we left the summit at about 1430 hrs. and stayed together for about two hours before Rick and Paula got bored and picked up their pace. I soloed the remainder of the trail and reached the Eyebrow Trail in just under three hours which meant that I would have to keep up my pace in order to reach the parking area before dusk. Well, I reached the trailhead at 1815 hrs. and found Rick waiting for me; Paula had departed a while before as she was somewhat concerned about driving in the dark. Rick and I changed into dry clothes and headed back home.

The Eyebrow

The Summit (center)

One of the easier sections of the trail

A pair of through hikers, she was from Nevada and he from Texas.

A view of the Umbagog, Mooselookmeguntic and Rangeley Lakes

It was a great day and we are looking forward to our next adventure, possibly North and South Crocker, Redington and Sugarloaf – we're keeping our fingers crossed for good hiking weather for the rest of September and the month of October. If snow holds off we may be fortunate enough to hike into November.

TEN MORE TO GO!

10, 9, 8, 7, 6, 5, 4, 3, 2, DONE!

AND THEN THERE WERE SEVEN

The weather for the week of September 9th looked like we could squeeze in a couple more peaks; I had an appointment early on Monday the 9th, but had the rest of the week pretty much clear. I called Rick on Sunday and the plan was for him to hike Mt. Ellen in Vermont, then meet me in Lisbon and then drive to Stratton, Maine to add South and North Crocker and Sugarloaf mountains to our inventory of completed four thousand footers.

We arrived in Stratton in the late afternoon and checked in to the Mountain View Motel on the Carrabassett Road in Stratton, about five miles north of the road to the trailhead. A word about the motel is appropriate here. The facility is owned and operated by Mark and Cindy Rollins; Mark was away on a fishing trip in Canada but in his absence Cindy took very good care of us.

We had a second floor end unit that included a living room, full kitchen, two bedrooms and bath, in addition we had a wide screen TV and air-conditioning.

The location was perfect. We were no more than five miles from the Caribou Valley Road where our trailheads were located, and two restaurants, general store and convenience store/gas station were just a few minutes' drive.

Living Room

Kitchen

Bedroom

We went to bed early Monday evening after having dinner at the White Wolf Inn, the only restaurant open in Stratton that evening. Actually, we were rather fortunate to have had any dinner at all; we had checked in at the motel at about 1945 hrs.; Cindy then informed us that the restaurant stopped serving at 2000 hrs. I immediately called and asked if they would stay open for another ten or fifteen minutes – they responded in the affirmative, so off we went to nourish our bodies for the following day.

We awoke at about 0530 hrs. and were at the trailhead within an hour. The trailhead to South Crocker (4.050') and North Crocker (4,228') is located about four and one-half miles from Route 16/27 on the Caribou Valley Road, a rough gravel road that eventually ends at Caribou Pond. The AMC Maine Mountain Guide described the trailhead as 4.3 miles from the main road; however, at about 3.8 miles the road was blocked with concrete barriers and it was necessary to add another mile to our trip log for the day.

Almost always the trailheads are identified with a sign and mileage. In this case there was no sign even though there are two AT (Appalachian Trail) trailheads directly across from each other; it really wasn't difficult to identify the trail because of the distinctive AT white trail markers on rocks about two or three meters in from the road.

Rick at the Trailhead (note the arrow pointing to the trail)   **Me at the Trailhead**

From the trailhead the distance to South Peak is 2.1 miles with an elevation gain of about 1,800 feet. The first mile consists of relatively easy grades but after passing the Crocker Cirque Trail junction the trail begins to steepen until it reaches the rocky shoulder of the mountain, from there the distance to the summit is about one-half mile. The summit is completely wooded but there is a short trail to a lookout about ten meters from the summit sign.

We were somewhat surprised to see a half dozen covered packs at the summit. Later the owners arrived and identified themselves as members of the Maine Conservation Corps; they had been in the mountains for several days.

        Me at the Summit   **Rick at the Summit**

Although the forecast was for rain in the morning and scattered thunderstorms in the afternoon, we were fortunate that we only encountered brief showers on the ascent – after a short rest at the summit we headed to the North Peak, a mile distant. The "book" time for the hike to the North Peak was forty-five minutes; Rick could have easily done it in that time but I took an hour and nine minutes for the hike.

We remained at the summit long enough to have a "through hiker" take our photos and then headed back to the South Peak for our descent. Although it did rain on the trip to the South Peak, it only rained for a short time and we encountered no thunder storms.

After we left the South Peak on our descent Rick picked up his pace. In about an hour, as I approached the Crocker Cirque Campsite junction, I thought I heard voices including his; in a short time he and other hikers came into view – hey, I recognize those hikers! What a coincidence. They were the same hikers that we met on Old Speck a week ago (see photo on page 175).

They had cellphones and we agreed to stand by for their call later in the afternoon and to meet them at the AT junction with Route 16 to take them into town for supplies, food and lodging. They never called and I don't know if they found a spot pitch their tent or not – in any event, we had rain and thundershowers during the night. They had been on the trail for a few months and were well prepared for the weather so we weren't overly concerned.

We made good time back to the car and the motel – I was happy to get first bid at the shower after which I changed clothes and relaxed on the sofa watching TV while Rick showered and got ready to head out for dinner.

The White Wolf Inn was closed on Tuesday so we ate at the restaurant directly across the road; the food was good but the music was loud! After dinner we headed back to the motel and watched TV until I turned in around 2200 hrs.

After a good night's rest we awoke a little later than we had the day before but were on the trail by 0800 hrs. Today our target would be Sugarloaf Mountain (4,250'), the second highest mountain in the state.

This trail was also part of the AT but a little more of a challenge. In just a short distance we had to cross the South Branch of the Carrabassett River which was a little higher than normal because of the rains the night before.

As we looked around for a suitable place to cross we noticed that someone had placed an eight foot plank across two rocks; although it was a help, one slip would have ended our day of hiking.

Here I am making my way to the "bridge". Rick made the crossing with no problem and I soon followed – OK, but just a little shaky.

Here's Rick with a demonstration of the sturdiness of our crossing facility.

After our successful river crossing, the trail rose gradually as it followed the river for a distance of about a half-mile. It was during this time that Rick picked up his pace – I did not see him again until I reached the junction of the AT and the spur to the summit, about two miles distant.

It wasn't long before the trail turned east and became considerably rockier and steeper; for me the going was slow.

It has been said that a picture is worth a thousand words. However, the only way to get an accurate description of the difficulty here is to experience it – words, at least for me, fall far short.

The trail continues steep and rocky until it reaches the 3,500 foot contour where it becomes more gradual until about a quarter mile from the spur intersection. Actually, there are sections that are a very pleasant "walk" through the woods – unfortunately, these sections are few.

The distance to the summit spur is 2.3 miles and the "book" time is two hours. Rick made it in just about book time but it took me four hours to make the same distance – OK laugh, but let me know how you do when you reach age 77.

Rick showed up shortly after I reached the intersection and informed me that he had already been to the summit. Although I was almost an hour ahead of my estimated time, it was obvious to me that the hike down was going to take me a lot longer – I am very careful on the rocky trail going up but much more careful on the way down.

Accordingly, I was concerned that I may not reach the trailhead on the way down before dark – I did not want to be on this trail after dark even though I had lights.

So I made the decision to give Rick the car keys and I would take the ski area utility road down from the summit to the base house in the Carrabassett Valley. Although the road was a bit longer, it would be easier for me to negotiate and, even if I had to hike a way in the dark, it would not have presented any difficulty for me.

So, we parted company at the spur junction. I made my way to the summit and Rick headed down to the parking area.

The distance to the summit via the spur is one-half mile; book time is thirty minutes, Rick made it in about half that time and it took me almost an hour. The views from the summit were wonderful but the wind was howling a gale. I spent about thirty minutes there before heading down the rough, gravel utility road.

Here is a view from the summit facing east, the peak in the center of the photograph is Burnt Hill (3,609').

The summit has several buildings, a couple of which serve the ski area and the chairlifts; the others serve towers that are burdened with microwave relay and cell antennae.

This is the official summit cairn.

My self-portrait at the Summit   **Rick's**

After a half hour or so at the summit I began to make my way down the access road; it was somewhat steep in places and very gravely so, even though it was a travelable road, caution was still necessary. In about two miles I reached a building where carpenters were working, I rested here for a few minutes before moving on. I walked for another mile or so and heard a vehicle coming up from the opposite direction - soon I saw an ATV (All Terrain Vehicle) and thought that it might be a ski area vehicle making a routine inspection. As the vehicle drew closer I could read the words "POLICE" on the front, I kept on walking still assuming that it was a routine patrol. After a few moments the vehicle stopped next to me and an attractive young police officer smiled and asked how I was doing. I replied that I was doing quite well and we chatted for a couple of minutes before she told me that she was actually looking for me.

HUH? I wondered why and then she told me that Rick had stopped by the police station and told them that I was coming down the utility road – he also told them that I was an experienced hiker and that there was really no concern. However; they decided to send an officer up the road to see how I was doing.

I truly appreciate Rick's concerns for my welfare but sometimes he is just a tad overprotective (see Page 46). After a brief discussion the police officer (Courtney) offered the option of having me continue on foot or giving me a ride on the ATV. The AMC requires that all hikes must be on foot both on the ascent and descent for the mountain peak to count – so, I weighed the facts:

a) The trail to the summit was 2.9 miles.
b) The elevation at the start of the hike was just about two thousand feet.
c) I had already hiked the utility road in excess of three miles.
d) And I was below the two thousand foot contour.
e) A very attractive young lady had just offered me a ride.

IT WAS REALLY A NO-BRAINER!

7, 6, 5, 4, 3, 2, DONE!

FIVE REMAINING

The week of September 24th looked favorable for bagging three more peaks, Spaulding (4,010'), Abraham (4,050') and Redington (4,010'). Rick and I planned to meet at the Mountain View Motel in Stratton on Tuesday afternoon; we would check in and then briefly explore the trailhead to the two Bigelow Peaks for a future hike. We then headed into town and picked up some supplies for our hike along with some sandwiches for dinner.

We both turned out of bed the following morning at about 0500 hrs. and headed for the Sugarloaf Ski Area - the plan was to ascend via the utility road and then proceed to the AT via the spur trail. When we reached the summit the wind was blowing between forty-five and fifty MPH, the visibility was about fifty meters and the wind chill was about freezing – there was ice at the summit.

We headed toward the spur trail as quickly as possible and once down in the trees it seemed almost summer-like even though the temperature was in the thirties.

The hike to the AT junction took me about twenty-five minutes and I found Rick waiting for me when I arrived; he had made the half-mile distance in about fifteen minutes.

We rested for a few minutes before heading southwest along the ridge between Mts. Sugarloaf and Spaulding. The distance from the AT/Sugarloaf Spur junction to the Mt. Spaulding Spur was 1.9 miles; from there it was just a short distance to the summit of Mt. Spaulding. The summit here was completely treed, and although there was a very short side trail to a viewpoint, there was nothing to be seen because we were totally in the clouds.

Here is the Dynamic Duo at the summit – look at the faces; are we having fun yet?

At the base of the spur we met two "through hikers" and another hiker seeking to complete the New England Four Thousand Footers as we were doing. After breakfast on Thursday we saw the two "through hikers" in town, they had decided to take a short break.

After a brief discussion with our fellow hikers and the photo session we again headed southwest toward Mt. Abraham. The distance to the summit spur is 1.9 miles but the trail descends over fourteen hundred feet before reaching the Mt. Abraham side trail to the summit (in mountaineering remember that whatever goes down must go up). Rick was nowhere in sight and I didn't have any idea how far ahead he was until much later.

When I reached the AT/Mt. Abraham summit spur I took off my pack and rested for a few minutes and shortly thereafter a pair of "through hikers" appeared – we chatted for a few minutes and I described the camping facility on the trail to South Crocker; they were considering remaining overnight there.

We parted and I headed up the summit side trail; the distance to the summit is 1.7 miles and the elevation gain is about fifteen hundred feet. Based on the topographical chart the elevation gain is relatively gradual for the first mile or so. At that point there was a note from Rick – he was about an hour and twenty minutes ahead of me. From there the trail became a bit steeper but soon, and once above the tree line, things changed dramatically - I can imagine that at that point most hikers shout out HOLY S**T! What a huge Talus Field!*

We're going where? You mean up there? Way up there?

Of course it was necessary to go down before going up and we had to repeat that a few more times before reaching the summit.

Rocks are a difficult thing for me – sure, sixty years ago it would have been nothing and I would have skipped over those rocks like a mountain goat, but now?

It was going to be a loooong day.

*A slope formed by an accumulation of rock debris.

The long and short of it was that I finally made the summit; by then the weather had cleared a bit and the visibility had greatly improved.

There was a tower at the summit; I assume that it was a tower for the fire warden but there was no way in the world that either of us would venture up the access ladder. As a matter of fact I was afraid that it might tip over with the wind we were experiencing at the summit.

Here is a photo from the summit looking north northeast. That's Mt. Spaulding in the left center of the photo and Mt. Sugarloaf in the center.

The cable in the photo was acting as a support for the tower; however, the end was only wrapped around a small rock.

So, here we were at the summit and thinking about our trek back to Mt. Sugarloaf and the base lodge about twelve miles away and with a couple of good elevation gains and a whole bunch of rocks to get back to the tree line and trail. So, what's the alternative?

A review of the map and the description of the Fire Warden's Trail and further considering that when we arrived at the end of the trail a friend was willing to meet us and take us back to where my car was parked, it seemed pretty obvious the Plan "B" was in order.

So we called our friend to confirm that he was willing to pick us up at the trailhead and drive us back to the parking area where we had left the car. But first we had a mile or so of Talus Field to cross. Mt. Abraham's Talus Field covers three hundred and fifty acres, and is the 2nd largest Alpine Zone in Maine.

We saw no trail signs but followed numerous cairns above the tree line for a distance of about a mile before we turned generally southeast, descended and entered the woods. The trail was well defined and descended gradually; according to the map we should end up on a dirt road, eventually cross a brook where there was a washed-out bridge, and continue to the parking area, only a short distance away.

After about an hour on the trail we came to a clearing where we could see Mt. Abraham; we stopped there for a few minutes and confirmed that we were heading in the right direction. It was getting dark but we still had good visibility and, although we had our headlamps, it wasn't necessary to turn them on at that time.

By the time we reached the dirt road it was dark and we used our headlamps and flashlights for the remainder of the adventure.

The road was a really nice road at least two rods wide and very well graded, we had a choice of going left or right but the left turn corresponded with the direction shown on our map. So we headed down in the dark but the road was smooth and the going was quite good. At one point I saw automobile headlights on my left and thought that perhaps it was our friend coming to pick us up.

We soon arrived at the brook and the washed-out bridge; just as described in the trail guide - wow, it won't be long before we reach the parking area and get back to the car.

We crossed the brook easily and climbed over the bridge abutment on the far side of the brook; from there the good road continued for a short distance before narrowing significantly. Rick decided to scout on ahead to see what he could before we moved on. He came back to my position about ten minutes later and reported that the trail turned slightly left and began to descend.

I called my wife Dawn on the cellphone and gave her our GPS coordinates – she told us that she could not see a travelable road anywhere near where we were. We did know that we were north of the town of Salem but did not know how far.

We continued on the trail until it became obvious that it was not a trail but most likely a skidder road for logging purposes. It was starting to get late and since we really didn't know now where we were, we decided to call to see if we could get some help. Our plan was to see if we could get the state police to locate us and let us know how we could get to the nearest road.

So, Rick called the state police on his I-Phone and they assured us that they knew where we were and told us that they were going to send game wardens out to get us. We told them we really didn't need to be rescued; all we needed was a confirmation as to where we were and a direction that would get us to the nearest travelable road – they insisted that they were going to send out the game wardens.

So now they started asking questions:

Are you both in good health?   YES

Do either of you have any medical problems?   NO

Do you have water, food, flashlights, compass, extra batteries, dry clothes, etc?   YES

Do you have a whistle?   YES*

Are you prepared, if necessary, to spend the night in the woods?   YES

But, we answered, even if we spend the night we still won't know where we are in the morning.

*A brief word about whistles. The AMC recommends that, among other necessary items, hikers carry whistles (and/or pepper spray); the primary reason is to ward off bears. Well, the truth is that I have never had a lot of faith in warding off bears with whistles, or even pepper spray for that matter, so I carry a short barrel stainless steel S & W .357 magnum as a more sensible and practical alternative. It has been my experience with bears that whistles do no more than tell them where you are. So, with my Smith & Wesson, I essentially have the equivalent of a whistle AND pepper spray.

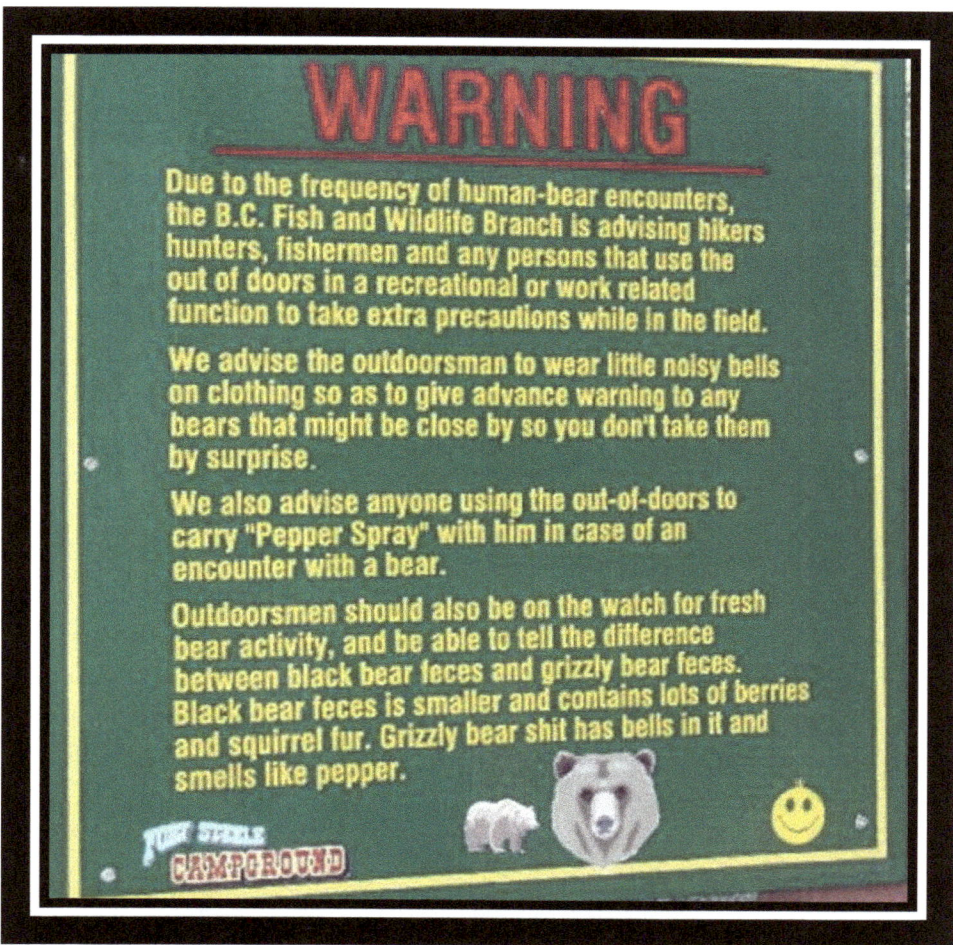

Above is a photo that I took several years ago of a sign on a trail in British Columbia. I include it here in support of my decision to carry an alternative to a whistle and pepper spray.

In a short while they called back and told us that they had contacted the wardens and they knew where we were – "….stay put and they'll be there as soon as they can…" Stay put? You've got to be joking – there was no way that the wardens could get to us in any kind of a vehicle.

So we decided to head back to the end of the road where the washed-out bridge was located; hell, if they could find the road they could find us.

Now the best part was that we had cell service and communication; we had spoken with Dawn numerous times and she was constantly aware of our movements. We soon received a call from the wardens who told us that they knew exactly where we were and they'd be along soon (hmm, didn't we just hear that?).

However, the GPS coordinates that the state police had given them was nowhere near where we were. When they had arrived at where they thought we were, they called and asked if we could see them. We replied "NO." Then they told us that they were going to turn on their sirens – "…can you hear them…?" Same answer: "NO." I suggested that they use OUR last known GPS coordinates, they agreed.

We made our way back to the washed-out bridge and waited to hear from the wardens – they soon called back and informed us that they **knew where we were**..... Uh huh! However, they told us that they were still about an hour away. They then asked if we were at the same location as the coordinates that we had given them – I answered that we were not, but were approximately fifty meters west of that location, which is well within the margin of GPS error. It was now after midnight.

The temperature was dropping and it was getting windy so they told us to build a fire if we could - well, we were at an ideal spot for a fire so arson Joe ordered Rick to get some birch bark and dry wood.

Birch bark is a fire starting miracle because it is waterproof and contains flammable oils and resins; Rick did a great job of finding both the bark and dry wood but needed a brief lesson in fire starting. I had told him about birch bark in past hikes so he attempted to light a piece that he had found – no luck. I explained that in some cases, particularly if the underside of the bark was still wet, it was necessary to gently peel off the top thin layer – I did this and got enough to assure me that we would be successful. I used a log as a backstop, put small dry wood sticks above the birch bark, carefully placed larger wood strips above the "kindling" making sure that there would be sufficient airflow, and lit a match – VOILA!

It wasn't long before we had a roaring blaze and also not very long before Rick decided to take full advantage of it:

Well Hell, I built it so I soon took advantage of it as well.

So, we had plenty of heat, food, water, communication, shelter and supplies for overnight if necessary; although we were not in an emergency situation it still would be nice to know how to get back to civilization. And, we were told, help was on the way.

So where did we go wrong? It's still a mystery. After sixty-five years of hiking, this was a first for me and although it was interesting and I am fully confident that we can survive in the woods in an emergency, I'll be just as happy if it never happens again.

At 0200 hrs. Rick spotted headlights coming around the bend above us – it was the wardens, and their first comment was that they had never "rescued" anyone with a fire like this one. The first thing was to put out the fire – after all that work, bummer! Then we packed our gear in one of the trucks and headed for Sugarloaf Ski Area.

Oooops, not so fast. We had traveled about two miles when Scott, our driver, slammed on the breaks and uttered: (expletive deleted) "……we have a flat tire!" So, Scott, Chris (the other warden) and Rick, under the watchful supervision of yours truly, went to work to replace the flat tire. I wanted to take photos but considered that discretion was the better part of valor.

It was a comedy of errors. This truck had its spare tire underneath and a special system for lowering it – after many futile attempts an instruction manual was referenced and within fifteen or so minutes the spare tire was in hand. During the first couple of attempts to raise the truck, it fell off the jack; another jack was located and that didn't work at first.

I had my camera with me and seriously thought about taking photos; however, I recalled that "discretion is the better part of valor".

Eventually, both jacks were put into service and the tire was successfully mounted. After about an hour we were back in business.

We followed the lumber road and eventually emerged onto Route 142 in Salem, soon we were back at Sugarloaf and shortly thereafter the weary hikers arrived at the motel, it was 0415 hrs. darned close to twenty-four hours after we had left.

Rick took a shower and then soaked his feet for a while before heading to bed – I skipped the shower and soaked my head in a couple of pillows, it was only a few nanoseconds before I was in dreamland.

Our original plan was to hike Mt. Redington the following day; however, it seemed prudent to put that off for our next adventure, hopefully soon.

5, 4, 3, 2 DONE

"Society speaks and all men listen, mountains speak and wise men listen." - Muir

We're now into October and the plan is to get all sixty-seven peaks done before the weather turns really cold with the possibility of snow in the upper elevations. A check of the weather reports for the Stratton area of Maine promised great weather for the week of the 1st.

So we headed out for Maine on Monday, the 30th and met at our favorite motel late that evening. Our two bedroom suite was unavailable that day so we shared a one bedroom unit for the one night; our unit would be available for the remainder of the week.

Our goal for the day was to hike the two four thousand foot peaks in the Bigelow Range, a 36,000 acre parcel established by referendum in 1976. The range is about twelve miles in length and is located about twelve miles south of Flagstaff Lake, a man-made lake with a surface area of 20,300 acres.

The lake is named after the town of Flagstaff, which was physically abandoned and dismantled in 1950 for the construction of the hydroelectric facility on the Dead River, thereby enlarging the existing Flagstaff Lake and submerging the abandoned town.

The Bigelow Range includes Cranberry Peak (3,194'), the Horns (3,792' & 3,805'), West Peak (4,145') and Avery Peak (4,088'); the latter two are the only four thousand footers in the range. Trail access is from the Carrabassett Road (Route 16/27); the AT trailhead is about a mile from the highway and the Fire Warden's trailhead is about a half mile further east.

The Fire Warden's Trail allows the shortest, but most steep access to the two peaks. The distance to the Bigelow Col and AT junction is 4.7 miles – from that point Avery Peak is 0.4 miles east and West Peak is 0.3 miles west. The trail is relatively easy for the first 3.6 miles before rising steeply beyond the Moose Falls Tentsite (2,500'). The elevation gain in the next mile is 1,500 feet.

In this photograph I am standing next to the hiker's registration box at the intersection of the Fire Warden's and Horn's Pond Trail, 1.7 miles from the trailhead.

It was at this point on the descent that we put on our headlamps, but I'm getting ahead of myself.

From this point on Rick surged ahead and I didn't see him again until I reached the Bigelow Col. I made the next distance (2 miles) in an hour and a half and was quite proud of myself; however, that came to a screeching halt as I started the steepest part of the climb.

At about the 3,500 foot contour I snapped a photograph of the west slope of Avery Peak – I later found out that this wasn't the summit!

I plodded on and when I estimated that I was at about two hundred feet below the Col I called Rick on the cellphone – naturally, he had been at the Col for a little over an hour and I was sadly behind schedule. He told me to turn off the phone and he would shout – OK, he shouted and I heard him! OK, I'm near the Col so the summits are not that far off – WRONG.

In a short while I joined Rick at the Col and we hiked a few minutes to the AT; Rick had already been to the Avery Peak so we decided to head west toward West Peak, 0.3 miles west; well, it was the furthest 0.3 miles that I can recall hiking; however, I can attest to the fact that the view was worth every agonizing step. The sky was virtually cloudless and the view was awesome!

The panoramic photograph above was taken by Rick. It looks north from the summit of West Peak over Flagstaff Lake – Canada can be seen in the distance.

Rick's self-portrait at the summit

Rick was able to get this photo of me at the summit.

The photo below shows Rick photographing the mountains to the south, he is standing about fifty meters from the actual summit.

We spent about fifteen or twenty minutes at the summit before heading back to the Col and the hike up to Avery Peak (right center).

Hey, it's less than a mile away so it must be a short hike, right? Uh huh….

We made our way back down to the Col, and decided to leave our packs at the caretaker's cabin and "slackpack" our way up to the summit of Avery.

And, while we're at the caretaker's cabin, how about a brief snooze? Worked for me!

All right, time to get up and get going - I'm hoping to get to the summit and back to the Col for the trip down no later than 1500 hrs.

We left the comfort of the cabin porch and headed up the rocky trail to the summit of Avery. Rick claimed that it had taken him fifteen or twenty minutes when he went up earlier – that meant that it would probably take me from thirty to forty-five minutes……it did.

At the summit we met a young lady and her dog – she lived nearby and frequently hiked solo. We chatted with her for a while and took a few photographs before heading back to the Col.

This photo is of me at the summit of Avery Peak; it is interesting to note that the narrow sign above the trail sign indicates that this is the two thousand mile marker of the Appalachian Trail from Springer Mountain, Georgia to Mount Katahdin in Maine, the sign informs "through hikers" that there are approximately two hundred miles left to travel before reaching the end.

About fifty meters east of the summit a stone foundation is all that remains of a former fire tower.

After a little too long at the summit we hiked back to the cabin, picked up our backpacks and started down – we were quite a bit behind schedule and it appeared that we would be hiking the lower part of the trail in the dark.

It was after 1600 hrs. when we headed down and I estimated that if we made relatively good time to the Moose Falls Tentsite we could be at the Horn's Pond Trail intersection before dark.

We arrived at the tentsite in pretty good time and I was confident that we could easily make the trail intersection without lights – we did! We had cell service there so I called Dawn to let her know our progress and we then prepared ourselves for the after dark adventure. We had 2.1 miles to travel before reaching the trailhead and, although more than half was rocky, the hike went quite well – we were pleased to finally reach the more level part of the hike which left about a mile of trail and a short river crossing before we reached the car.

Part of the trail followed the shores of Stratton Brook Pond and, although it was dark and we couldn't see them, we certainly heard the moose and knew that they were nearby – it was the rutting season and we really didn't want to disturb their natural instincts. We were hoping that if we left them alone they would leave us alone – we did and, thankfully, they did.

When we were within a half mile of the car we saw lights a short distance away; when we got closer we met three young women who were setting up a tent for an overnight stay. I stopped and chatted for a few minutes – the three were from New Hampshire and were working on the One Hundred Highest Peaks in New England. They had over seventy and were planning on hiking Sugarloaf, Spaulding and Abraham the following day. After that they planned to hike Redington. Our plan was to take a day of rest and hike Redington on Thursday.

I hiked on to find Rick already at the car – we headed back to the motel where we each took a nice hot shower and relaxed for a while before turning in. It was a long hard day and although the weather was ideal and the views were spectacular we were feeling the results of our efforts; however, a good rest and a day off would bring back our spirits and incentive to take on another peak.

Score: Sixty-four down……..Three to go!

During our rest day we drove to Rangeley to check out our final adventure. We found a reasonably priced motel located about fifteen minutes from the trailhead; the facility has a hot tub and swimming pool so it can't be all bad……..but that's getting ahead of the story.

Our next adventure would take place the following day with a hike up Mt. Redington.

After a good day's rest we awoke early and drove to the Caribou Pond Road, about five miles south of our motel. We followed the road 3.9 miles to where it had been blocked off and parked the car. This is the same parking place that we parked for our hikes to South and North Crocker and also for Sugarloaf. From there it was a three mile hike to the end of the road where our adventure would begin.

The summit of Mt. Redington was previously listed as 3,984 feet in elevation but in 2005 the Maine Mountain Power Company filed an application with the Maine Land Use Regulation Committee to construct a thirty turbine wind farm on the summit of Redington and nearby Black Nubble; at that time more sophisticated measuring devices were used and the official elevation changed to 4,010 feet.

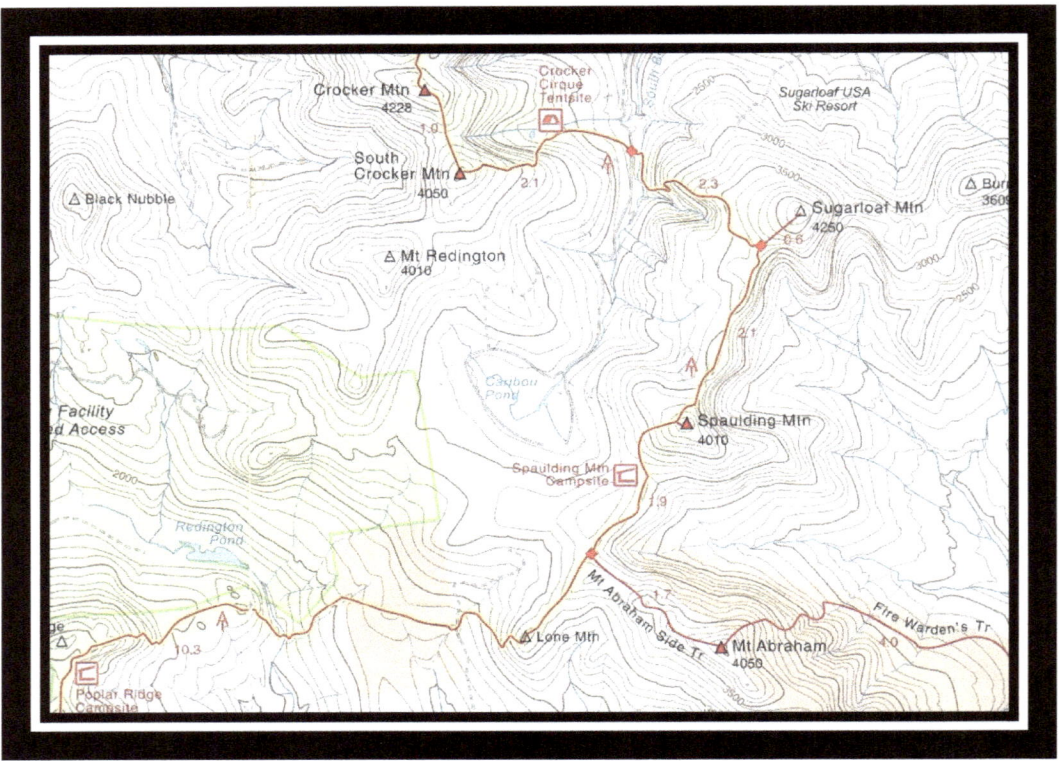

In 2007 the application for the wind turbine farm was turned down but the mountain soon gained popularity because it was now a four thousand footer; however, the challenge was that there was no maintained trail to the summit thereby making it one of the only two trail-less peaks on the four thousand foot list, the other being Owl's Head in New Hampshire (see page 103).

Although Mt. Redington is a trail-less mountain, there are essentially two frequently followed "routes" to the summit, a bushwhack from adjacent South Crocker Mountain or via the Caribou Pond Road, logging roads, herd paths and bushwhacking. We decided to take the latter, so with GPS coordinates from satellite photos we began our adventure.

The first three miles of our hike followed an old logging road along the north shore of the South Branch of the Carribassett River to a point where the road terminated at the mouth of Caribou Pond. From that point we hiked west on a rather well-defined logging road for another mile – it wasn't long before we saw our goal - what a beautiful sight.

That's Mt. Redington just right of center; the peak at the left is unnamed and although it appears higher it is only about 3,700 feet in elevation. This logging road travels west for about a mile and then turns north for another half-mile. The elevation here is about 2,800 feet which suggests that the elevation gain to the summit is just over 1,200 feet, the least elevation gain we've experienced thus far.

We turned north and hiked a half-mile to another logging road junction, all the time gaining gradually in elevation. So far my GPS coordinates were working out just fine and we were right on track.

Since there are no maintained trails, trail signs are not permitted; however, some helpful hikers have made rather crude signs of their own.

This one was made with sticks, a rock, and a ribbon.

This one was made with stones.

There were also numerous stone cairns; here is a combination of a stone cairn and wood arrow.

The lumber roads ended at the point where the photograph on the previous page was taken; from there the "trail" in some places was obvious and in other places it was not. This was the last spot where I had a GPS coordinate other than the summit itself.

Here is a photo that shows the trail as pretty obvious.

In this photo the trail is not quite as obvious – so, on the average, I'd guess about 50/50.

Rick reached the summit about twenty minutes before me and had successfully scouted around for the summit canister where hikers logged in, thereby proving that they had actually been there.

Although the canister contained two plastic containers with a small notebook and pens, I had previously typed out our information and laminated it. We did, however, make a note in the log that our information was just a tad in error – since we had planned to hike Redington a week before and since at that time it would have been peak #63, we corrected the error in the logbook.

The Dynamic Duo at the Summit Canister

Although the summit had been "cleared" relative to the investigation of a potential wind farm, there are still many trees remaining and the views are limited, particularly to the south.

There have been reports of trash left by the wind generator developers but I was pleased to find that it had been removed.

This photograph is facing north from the center of the summit clearing. I suppose that it would be possible to cut a "free" Christmas Tree' however, that would require driving to Maine hiking four hours to the summit, cutting a tree and carrying it back four hours to the car – and, possibly facing charges of illegal tree cutting.

This photo faces north; the mountains in the distance are probably in Canada. If you look very closely you will see about twenty-five or thirty wind generators on the hills before the mountain peaks.

We remained on the summit for about an hour before heading back down the trail; Rick decided to get down as quickly as he could while I decided to saunter along at my own pace and with several stops along the way to enjoy the scenery.

I met Rick at a flat area from which we had a beautiful view of Mt. Redington and where we could reflect on the day and the beauty of the area.

We spent another half hour or so just enjoying everything around us. The day could not have been more glorious.

From here we hiked the road back to the parking area and then headed back to the motel; we had hiked twelve miles in about ten hours. This hike was a gift from heaven. Every step of the hike, at least for me, was a joy – we couldn't have asked for a better day. Our only regret was having to leave.

We have now completed sixty-five out of the sixty-seven four thousand foot peaks in New England. God has been good to us and to me especially for letting me do what I do at my age; we both eagerly look forward to our final hike – Saddleback Mountain and the Horn, both in Rangeley, Maine.

"Keep close to Nature's heart….and break clear away, once in a while, and climb a mountain or spend a week in the woods, wash your spirit."

John Muir

2.....DONE!

SADDLEBACK MOUNTAIN AND THE HORN

"It is not the mountain that we conquer but ourselves."

Sir Edmund Hillary

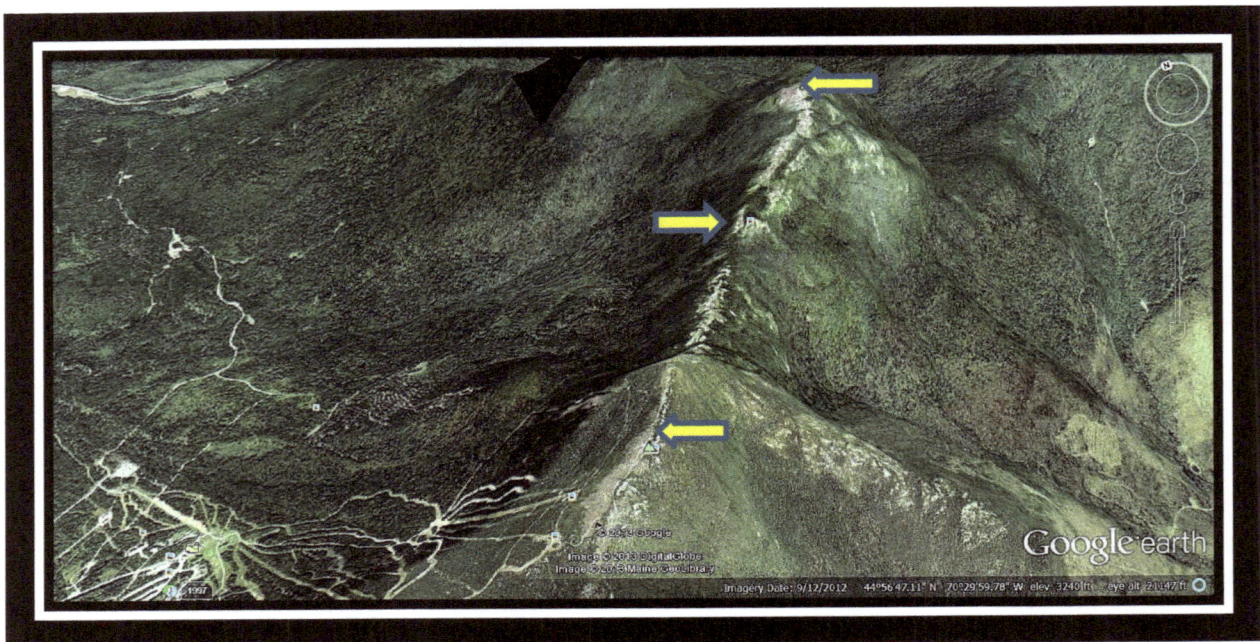

Satellite Image of Saddleback Mountain (lower Center), Ridge (center), The Horn (top center)

Our last venture in pursuit of the New England Four Thousand Footers took us to Rangeley, Maine and Saddleback Mountain (4,120') and The Horn (4,041'). Saddleback's long ridge extends in a general northeast-southwest direction for more than three miles; the Saddleback Mountain Ski Area is located on the northwest slope of the mountain (photo, lower left). Both peaks are bare and afford extensive three hundred sixty degree views; the distance between the two peaks is 1.7 miles and the trail dips approximately five hundred feet in the "saddle".

On October 9th Dawn and I headed to Rangeley, ME for an overnight at the Saddleback Inn, Rick planned to meet us that evening to review our hike scheduled for the following day. Dawn and I had finished dinner and had just returned to the room when Rick called to join us and discuss our plans. We agreed to meet at 0545 hrs. and drive to the Saddleback Ski Area, about fifteen minutes distant.

Saddleback Mountain and The Horn

The following morning was cold and by the time we were on the trail the sun was just beginning to appear and the color of the sky was awesome.

In this photograph the Rangeley Lakes and vicinity are enshrouded by early morning fog – by noon the fog had completely lifted.

There are several approaches to the Saddlebacks but we decided to ascend and descend via the Saddleback ski trails and join the Appalachian Trail near the summit of Saddleback Mountain.

The ascent begins at the Base Lodge and follows the Wheeler Slope, Gray Ghost and Tri Color ski trails to the Kennebago Quad - from where a trail leads to the intersection with the AT. The elevation gain is about sixteen hundred feet in a distance of approximately two and one-half miles. Although the trail is not marked it is pretty well worn and fairly easy to follow; I might add that, although these trails are shorter than the approach via the AT, they are not a "short-cut." The trails are "relentless" and steep right from the base lodge to the ledges above the Quad, the highest point of the ski trails – there is a first aid station located there.

The Quad

From the Quad a short trail through a wooded area emerges on the ledges southwest of the summit of Saddleback Mountain.

Saddleback Mountain Summit Marker

#66

The Dynamic Duo at the summit sign.

Rick is saying:

"Hey, the old man actually made it this far."

I'm saying:

"You're damned right! See you at the Horn. (I hope!!!)"

We are now on the Appalachian Trail (AT) and heading northeast toward the Horn, 1.7 miles away. In doing so we must descend one hundred feet, ascend one hundred feet to the next "hump", descend about six hundred feet to the base of the "saddle", and then ascend five hundred plus feet to the summit of the Horn.

The trail was steep and rocky in many places but there were also open and relatively flat ledge areas that were a welcome change from the former.

Most of the steeper rock ledges were relatively easy to negotiate but this one required assistance.

The photograph above was taken from the lower ledges just before descending into the lower part of the "saddle" – The Horn summit can be seen at the upper center. As we ascended the open ledges below the summit, we saw that someone had written "ALMOST" in rocks. Did that person mean almost to the summit of the Horn or almost to the end of the Appalachian Trail; if it was the latter, the distance to Mount Katahdin is still about two hundred and twenty miles.

The distance between Saddleback Mountain and the Horn is 1.7 miles, I was thrilled to make the 1.7 miles in two hours; Rick could have been over and back in that time.

WE DID IT!

#67

Now, of course, we have to do the whole thing over in reverse; our hope was to get back to the base lodge by 1700 hrs. We left the summit of the Horn at about 1230 hrs. and my plan was to be back at the Saddleback summit no later than 1500 hrs. But first:

The photograph above is looking from the ledges just below the summit of the Horn toward the summit of Saddleback Mountain – if you look carefully, (and slightly right of center) you will see Rick and a couple that we met on the summit of the Horn.

We arrived back at Saddleback earlier than we expected and called Dawn to meet me at the base lodge between 1700 and 1730 hrs.

In most instances, at least for me, it takes almost as much time to descend as it does to ascend, particularly if the trail is steep and rocky – naturally, it is somewhat faster because I don't require as many rest stops on the way down.

We stopped briefly at the Quad and then proceeded down to the next intersection where we met a couple of trail workers. This rest stop was at the top of the Royal Coachman Trail where there was a warming shed, the top of one of the chairlifts and a building that was evidently ancillary to the snowmaking apparatus. There was also a large sign depicting the ski trail system.

There was also a picnic table that made a great resting place. After a brief rest Rick picked up his pace a bit while I continued my own steady, but slower pace. Rick and I met at about the three thousand foot contour and in view of the base lodge – a time check suggested that we would be at the lodge before our estimated time. As we continued I watched for Dawn and when we were about one hundred meters from the base I spotted her coming up the trail toward us.

What better way to end the day?

I've hiked a lot of mountains over the past sixty-five years and it's not hard to imagine that some were more difficult than others, but as Sir Edmund Hillary said: *"It is not the mountain that we conquer but ourselves."* There is a lot to be said for that statement. God tests us in many different ways and frequently places obstacles in our path to see how we handle adversity. The key to success, at least in my view, is to face each challenge with a positive attitude and to ask God for the strength to continue - even though the challenge appears impossible, at least at first blush. I have had this thought numerous times during recent hikes; however, I may be slow but I have never, and as long as I am physically able, will never quit.

Oswald Chambers stated it well in **My Utmost for His Highest** when he said:

"God is the master designer, and He allows adversities into your life to see if you can jump over them…..Rise to the occasion. Do what the trial demands of you. It does not matter how much it hurts as long as it gives God the opportunity to manifest the life of Jesus in your body."

So, the bottom line is that I will continue to hike as long as God allows me to do so; each mountain is a challenge and each time I conquer a new peak I, as Sir Edmund said, conquer myself. I pray that God will continue to smile on my hiking activity.

EPILOGUE

It's been six months since we completed the last of the New England Four Thousand Footers and, although we've not done any serious mountaineering, we have done some modest exercising. Now that spring has made its way into southern New England, Rich has temporarily set his sights on the 92 mile Mid-State Trail which extends from the Rhode Island border to New Hampshire. I have done some local walking and have hiked Mt. Willard numerous times during the winter months, but so-far spring has successfully eluded northern New Hampshire.

However, on the 12th of April, the long-awaited AMC Four Thousand Footer Club Award Ceremony finally arrived. I hadn't seen Rich in person since October and I looked forward to seeing him again and reviewing some of our goals for the upcoming season. Dawn agreed to attend with me.

We met Rich outside and since I had already checked us all in, we went right over to the booth where our friends Nancy and Pat were selling their book *Its Not About the Hike*. It was great seeing them again and we looked forward to another of Nancy's DVDs with all of the photos submitted with membership applications.

The award ceremony started and the auditorium was packed with five hundred enthusiastic hikers, families and friends. The White Mountain Four Thousand Footer group was called first and each recipient got applause and yells from the crowd. Then came the New England Four Thousand foot group; that's the group that Rich and I were in.

Rich received his award first and when I tried to get a photo, my camera would not cooperate –

but we did get a photo later. My name was eventually called and the moderator also announced that I was the oldest member to get the award this year – more applause and hoots and hollers. This is the second year in a row that I've been the oldest member to receive an award, last year it was the White Mountain Four Thousand Footer Award and this year it was the New England Four Thousand Footer Award – a habit perhaps? I hope so.

Here I am receiving the award from committee member Sue Eilers.

The Award   Rich and I after the Ceremony

Rich and I with Committee Member Keith D'Alessandro

So, awards in hand, what's next? Well, the AMC Four Thousand Footer Club website, http://www.amc4000footer.org/, had the following dialogue along with my photograph: "*Dr. Nyberg was this year's oldest finisher for the NE67. And last year, he was the oldest finisher for the WM48. Here's hoping the trend continues next year, for the NE100!*" Hmmm, New England 100 Highest…it sounds like a possibility for another adventure, but that's long-range planning for the old guy.

Record of New England Four Thousand Foot Peaks

VERMONT   COMPLETE   Dr. Leonard J. Nyberg, Jr.

Mountain	Elevation	Date	Companion
Mt. Abraham	4,006	7/12/2013	Rick
Camel's Hump	4,083	*	Mary-Jo Nyberg, Ron Parker, Solo
Mt. Ellen	4,083	6/15/2013	Solo
Killington Peak	4,235	7/17/2013	Rick
Mt. Mansfield/Chin	4,393	**	Mary-Jo Nyberg with our two dogs.
* When I was a member of the Green Mountain Club I took care of the Montclair Glenn Shelter. I have hiked Camel's Hump many times during summer and winter from 1969 to 1973			
** I hiked Mt. Mansfield with my wife and our two German Shepherd dogs during the summer of 1970 - I did not keep a date log at that time.			

MAINE   COMPLETE

Mountain	Elevation	Date	Companion
Mt. Abraham	4,050	9/26/2013	Rick
Bigelow - Avery	4,090	10/1/2013	Rick
Bigelow - West Peak	4,145	10/1/2013	Rick
Crocker Mtn.	4,228	9/10/2013	Rick
Crocker Mtn. - South	4,050	9/10/2013	Rick
Katahdin - Baxter	5,268	*	Ray Barrie
Katahdin - Hamlin	4,756	**	Mary-Jo Nyberg
North Brother	4,151	7/31/2013	Rick
Old Speck	4,170	9/4/2013	Rick
Redington	4,010	10/3/2013	Rick
Saddleback	4,120	10/10/2013	Rick
Saddleback - Horn	4,041	10/10/2013	Rick
Spaulding	4,010	9/26/2013	Rick
Sugaroaf	4,250	9/11/2013	Rick
* I first hiked Katahdin when I was in high school, sometime during the summer of 1954, my hiking companion was Ray Barrie (see Volume I at page 5).			
** I hiked Katahdin again and included Hamlin with my wife during the summer of 1965.			

NEW HAMPSHIRE

COMPLETE   I am a current member of the AMC Four Thousand Footer Club

Record of New England Four Thousand Foot Peaks

Richard J. Arsenault, Jr.

VERMONT   COMPLETE

Mountain	Elevation	Date	Companion
Mt. Abraham	4,006	7/12/2013	Joe
Camel's Hump	4,083	*	
Mt. Ellen	4,083	6/15/2013	Solo
Killington Peak	4,235	7/17/2013	Joe
Mt. Mansfield/Chin	4,393	*	

* I hiked Mt. Mansfield and Camel's Hump with my cousin Andrew in July, 1988.

MAINE

Mountain	Elevation	Date	Companion
Mt. Abraham	4,050	9/26/2013	Joe
Bigelow - Avery	4,090	101/2013	Joe
Bigelow - West Peak	4,145	10/1/2013	Joe
Crocker Mtn.	4,228	9/10/2013	Joe
Crocker Mtn. - South	4,050	9/10/2013	Joe
Katahdin - Baxter	5,268	*	
Katahdin - Hamlin	4,756	*	
North Brother	4,151	7/31/2013	Joe
Old Speck	4,170	9/4/2013	Joe
Redington	4,010	10/3/2013	Joe
Saddleback	4,120	10/10/2013	Joe
Saddleback - Horn	4,041	10/10/2013	Joe
Spaulding	4,010	9/26/2013	Joe
Sugaroaf	4,250	9/11/2013	Joe

* I hiked both Mt. Katahdin and Hamlin Peak with my cousin Andrew in July, 1988.

NEW HAMPSHIRE

COMPLETE   I am a current member of the AMC Four Thousand Footer Club

ACKNOWLEDGMENTS

Page 24 -   The Geology of the White Mountains – after Creasy, 1974; Osberg et al, 1978
Page 25 -   From The Geology of New Hampshire by Marland P. Billings
Page 75 -   Sign on the wall of the AMC Lakes of the Clouds Hut
Page 85 -   East Branch and Lincoln RR Map – www.whitemountainhistory.org
Page 86 -   AMC Trail Map – 1934 White Mountain Guide Book
Page 87 -   Portion of White Mountains Trail Map – www.mapadventures.com
Page 112 - White Mountain Images – www.whitemountainimages.org
Page 116 - Portion of White Mountains Trail Map – www.mapadventures.com
Page 146 - Burlington (VT) Free Press
Page 151 - National Weather Service – Burlington, VT
Page 167 - Baxter State Park location map
Page 169 - Portion of Maine AMC Trail Map
Page 174 - United States Weather Service – Old Speck Mountain
Page 175 - Google Earth Satellite Image
Page 197 - Trail Sign – British Columbia Fish and Wildlife Branch
Page 201 - Portion of Maine AMC Trail Map
Page 208 - Portion of Maine AMC Trail Map
Page 216 - Google Earth Satellite Image
Page 226 - Facebook.com/Benefits Of Giving